Fun Nosework for Dogs

Teach your dog to enjoy using his nose!

by Roy Hunter

— Second Edition —

D1451005

HOWLN MOON PRESS

Fun Nosework for Dogs

By Roy Hunter
First Edition © 1995
Second Edition © 2003

Illustrated by Judi Duffy

Published by: Howln Moon Press
7222 State Highway 357, Franklin, NY 13775
1-607-829-2187

ISBN 1-888994-03-7
Printed and bound in the United States

Sixth Printing September 2006

Library of Congress Cataloging-in-Publication Data

Hunter, Roy.
  Fun nosework for dogs : teach your dog to enjoy using his nose! / Roy Hunter.
    p. cm.
  ISBN 1-888994-03-7 (alk. paper)
    1. Search Dogs — Training. 2. Tracking Dogs — Training. 3. Dogs — Training. I. Title.
SF429.73.H85 1998
636.7'0886 — dc21

97-46889
CIP

Acknowledgements

I would like to thank all those who inspired me to write this book, and all the people in the past who have contributed to my knowledge. I would especially thank Alan Cole for his continued support in this book and my other ventures.

I would also like to thank Judi Duffy for the light-hearted line drawings that illustrate this book. They are in keeping with the attitude I believe should be used in teaching 'Fun Things'. — *Roy Hunter*

Cover illustration and book design by Howln Moon Press.

"In order to really enjoy a dog, one doesn't merely train him to be semi-human. The point of it is to open oneself to the possibility of becoming partly a dog."
— Edward Hoagland

About Roy Hunter

Roy Hunter knows a little something about dogs. Even after forty years with them, he is quick to tell you that he is not an expert and he is still

learning from all the people and dogs who flocked to his classes, seminars, courses and games days near his home in Stambourne, England and throughout Britain.

Retired from the Metropolitan Police Force in London after twenty-five years (sixteen in the Dog Section—at one time Deputy Chief Instructor at the largest Police Dog Establishment in Europe), Roy finished his fifteenth consecutive year coming to the US in 1998.

Roy tracking with his German Shepherd, Tim.

Roy has given seminars all over the world on all types of dog training from Police Work, Obedience Instructor's Courses, Nosework Courses, Fun and Games, Agility, Competitive Obedience (he is a Working Trials Judge)... you name it!

In 1995 he published his first book in the United States—***Fun and Games with Dogs***. Continuing in the same style of having fun with your dog, Roy has added ***Fun Nosework for Dogs*** so that you too can teach your dog to enjoy using his amazing nose... Look for Roy's other popular books: ***MORE Fun and Games with Dogs*** and ***FUNctional Dog Training***... all published by Howln Moon Press.

Table of Contents

Introduction to the Second Edition

It has already been seven years since the first publication of **Fun Nosework** in the United States (eight in the United Kingdom) and I have been tremendously gratified to find it still going strong! It proves to me that many handlers are really interested in having FUN with their dogs as well as applying some of the information to real life situations such as search and rescue. It has been my privilege to share some of the ideas I have learned along the way with the many people and dogs that continue to show interest in all kinds of nosework.

In this edition, I have included more games with scent, a description of the figure eight style of tracking harness (as requested by many), additional information on scent discrimination using your own body, and some background on tracking hard surfaces — which is becoming more popular as new information is learned about this complex subject.

In all nosework, the dog is great at doing his own thing, but when we are trying to get him to use this ability for our own purpose, the position is delicately balanced. If we chastise the dog (however mildly) because we have not made our desires clear, then we may very well put the dog off for a long while. Both the dog and handler should be having FUN; a dog should NEVER associate any form of nosework with disagreeable experiences! Handlers must not show impatience... if you are in a bad mood, feeling unwell or just not yourself, do not indulge in any form of dog training until you are once again in a cheerful mood.

We humans are lucky to share our lives so deeply with another species. Treat your canine friend with the love and respect a dog deserves, and you will be rewarded tenfold. — *Roy Hunter, 2003*

Introduction to Nosework (from the First Edition)

I am writing this book as a result of many requests from dog people who have been on my "Nosework Course". Hopefully, this will open many eyes to the fun and enjoyment that this natural ability can bring to both humans and dogs.

The dog's sense of smell exceeds our own to a degree that is unimaginable. We can only touch the surface of this incredible ability. To demonstrate the difference between a human's olfactory organs and those of a dog, one friend of mine compares a large pocket handkerchief with a postage stamp displayed in one corner. He might be near to being correct—who knows? I have also heard figures of 1,000 to 1 quoted. Where do people get these figures? I prefer to simply say that a dog's sense of smell is vastly superior to ours.

A dog's whole world is mainly experienced through the nose, whereas ours is shown to us by our eyes. Although we each use other senses, these are ancillary to the primary sense. If a dog's sense of smell is compared to our sense of sight, some idea of the dog's ability may be understood. We can see shapes, sizes and colors at a glance—even those a long distance away. A dog can distinguish various smells even though they are (to us) very old or faint, and also when the source of the scent is a long distance away from the dog.

Glen Johnson, an English born Canadian, was and continues to be the world's leading exponent of 'nosework'. He taught German Shepherd Dogs to find leaks in the gas pipes under the sidewalks of New York. His dogs and handlers also found gas leaks in pipes stretching ninety miles across Canada and buried deep in the ground. In the United States, he taught dogs to find the eggs of the Gypsy Moth. (A moth whose caterpillars decimated hundreds of square miles of forest.) These eggs would never have been found by humans without the aid of the dogs. This enabled the authorities to know exactly which areas to spray. I learned a lot through listening to him although at the time I had already been instructing Police Dog handlers for some years.

Service dogs find drugs, explosives and the causes of arson. Dogs have been used to find copper ore in the mountains of Australia. A dog in New Zealand could locate six inch nails under six feet of water. I trained a Rottweiler to indicate a scented cloth from ten other plain ones. The scented cloth had been wrung out after being dipped into water to which one drop of peppermint essence had been added to forty gallons of water. The other cloths had been wrung out after being dipped in plain water. Unfortunately, the Customs Service never required a peppermint searching dog! This same dog could also discriminate between water that came out of the hot water faucet from that coming out of the cold water faucet. (The difference being that the cold water was run in lead pipes and the hot water in copper.)

In the wild environment, a dog would hunt for his food in basically two ways: he would locate and follow the footprints of his prey with his nose (tracking), OR he would smell the scent of his quarry in the air (air scenting). The latter is sometimes call 'wind scenting'—even though on a still day there is no wind. The wind makes it easier for the dog when it is downwind of the prey. It also makes it harder when the dog is upwind of the prey. We must always bear this in mind when working the dog. Even if there is no actual wind blowing, air currents may be moving due to weather and ground conditions. For example: on a slope during hot weather, scent will be carried upwards on a still day.

On the "Nosework Course", I teach tracking, searching for articles bearing human scent, searching for humans, and various aspects of scent discrimination. We will cover this and more. I hope all readers have FUN with this book. The contents apply for all kinds of dogs—from the beloved family pet to the serious work of service dogs.

Enjoy nosework, enjoy yourself, enjoy your dog!

Photo courtesy Howln Moon Press © 2003

Basic Nosework Training

We do not actually teach a dog to track, or to use his nose in any other way. What we do is harness the dog's natural instincts and abilities for our own purposes and train the dog to make use of these skills where and when we want. There are five rewards we can give a dog for doing what we want. I call these the Five P's because they all begin with the letter P.

1. **Praising**: this is verbal. Speak to your dog in a kind and affectionate manner. The TONE of your voice is important, not the actual words.

2. **Petting**: this is physical. Use a long gentle stroke, fondle, or touch. Patting, thumping or short, brisk strokes are irritating and not considered petting by my definition!

3. **Popping**: this means popping a small delicious treat into the dog's mouth. Treats MUST be something the dog loves, not just likes—or not just something you think the dog should love! Experiment to find out what your dog enjoys. I once knew an Afghan that loved dry bread—which was cheap and easy for the handler...

4. **Playing**: this means literally playing with your dog. Let yourself go—there are many ways to play with a dog: some involve toys (chase a ball, tug-of-war), some involve your own movement (running with your dog is a form of play).

5. **Pleasant** Expression: Dogs are much better than we are in reading our facial expressions and body postures. They know we smile when we are in a good mood and when we frown or scowl we are unpleasant to be around.

In NOSEWORK, the most important P's are popping (finding food) and playing (after finding something or someone). I advocate using the following three methods of training which can be used side-by-side in the same training session.

> • **Inducive**—*we get our dog to **want to do something** (for us) by using a lure (food, toys)...*
>
> • **Compulsive**—*we **guide** the dog into doing what we want (not to confused with force training) by showing the dog what is wanted...*
>
> • **Spontaneous**—*when a dog is doing something we approve of, we put a name to it and we use that word (sound) each time the dog **does the action on his own** until the association is formed in the dog's mind. Eventually the dog will perform the desired action when we use that word and then we can reward him—and the association will be made stronger...*

If you use compulsion (guiding) or inducement (a lure), commands are not to be introduced to the dog in any exercise until the dog readily accepts the exercise. If you introduce a command while the dog is resisting, it will give the dog a negative feeling towards the exercise AND the command itself! Training sessions should be short so that the dog does not become bored or stressed. All animals (including humans) will repeat an action they find rewarding... **so make it rewarding**!

If, for some reason, your dog does not respond to my methods, DO NOT give up! There are many good books available with other ideas which may work for you... as long as both you and your dog are having FUN.

It is very helpful (but not always necessary) to have a dog that will retrieve. If you have a dog that retrieves now, great. If you want to teach your dog to retrieve, see the Appendix in the back of this book. Teaching a dog to alert (speak) when they find something or someone is very handy too—I have included a section on that as well. I outline other "games" too to help develop your dog's drive and willingness. Try to teach them to your dog separately from (and before trying) nosework. All of them will enhance your enjoyment of your dog.

Scent Discrimination

Identifying Individual Humans

Just as humans (apart from the colorblind) can tell at a glance if an item is red, blue or green, OR if an article is round, square or oblong, so a dog can tell if an item has been handled by person A, B, C... or all the way through Z. Dogs can distinguish between one scent and another and correctly identify who has handled what.

In competitions here in Great Britain, the dog has to find his handler's scent on a cloth among other cloths that bear no human scent. Later in competitions and in training, the dog also finds a cloth bearing his handler's scent from among other cloths—some of which have been handled by a third party. In the hardest competition, the dog must find the Judge's scent on a cloth among other cloths—some of which have been handled by a third party. In the USA, the dog has to find an article that has just been freshly handled by the person working him in competition from among several others that have been handled on previous occasions by the same person—that is, to find the "hottest" scent.

In a practical application, some Police Forces use the dog's amazing sense of smell to identify a suspect (from among several innocent people) when a housebreaking instrument or a weapon was found at the scene of a crime. This is carried out in a similar fashion to an identity parade. I saw this demonstrated in Holland over thirty years ago and had wanted to introduce it to the Metropolitan Police Force in London. Had the Chief Instructor at that time been more open minded, perhaps more crimes would have been solved... Never mind!

My own method of training scent discrimination was devised because I realized the similarity of the dog's primary sense (smell) with our own (sight). We do not have to prolong a stare at an item to identify it; a dog does not have to have the scent forced on him for a length of time to be able to recognize it on something else—even if the smell is very faint.

Training Scent Discrimination

Choose a half dozen easily retrievable articles and put them out in the garden to air. (If you put them in a 4' x 4' wooden frame that is 2" high, you can contain them in one area.) (See Diagram.) Take one article out of the

box and throw it a few times (away from the box) for the dog to retrieve. Praise and love him up when he does so.

Stand (with the dog) about three yards away from the box. Throw the article so that it lands beside the box. (See Diagram.) Send the dog and praise him lavishly when he returns with it.

Next, throw it into the box and send the dog after it immediately. If he retrieves the same article, praise lavishly again. If he goes to pick up the wrong one, say "UGH" gently. Even if he brings the wrong one back, **do not tell him**

off. Just take it from him and put it away somewhere, but NOT back in the box. Go back one stage and try again. The first time you see him using his nose to identify the article, praise while he is sniffing the right one. After that, you must **never** praise him while he is investigating—he only gets praised when he has come right back to you with the article. The reason for this is that if he is ever unsure and has always previously been praised when he is right for sniffing the correct one, he will rely on your praise to reassure him. **So remember— he only gets praised for sniffing the right article the first time you start to train this discipline**! He also only gets told UGH the first time he goes to pick up the wrong article. If he comes back with the wrong one, take it from him and put it away. Give him your scent once more, and send him again.

Once you are throwing the article into the box, you will need to get into the habit of 'giving the dog your scent' before you send him. He doesn't really need this when he is looking for an article bearing your OWN scent, but eventually you may want him to find articles bearing the scent of other people. Then, he will need to know which scent he is looking for... and by 'giving him the scent' right from the beginning, he will know what is required of him and the introduction will not have been changed.

Giving scent is not a complicated exercise. **Just as you can distinguish between colors, sex, shapes, etc. at a glance, so can a dog at a sniff**. Just hold your hand one inch from his nose for only two or three seconds before sending him to retrieve. (See Diagram.) You will see people in obedience competitions practically suffocating the dog to insure that he really got the scent. It really is unnecessary and in some cases proves to be counterproductive.

You will find that your dog realizes what is required very quickly. Once he is reliable about bringing back the correct article thrown into the box, then begin to pause awhile before sending him. When this stage is okay, throw the article and turn the dog around in a circle before sending him (do not make this an exact circle of 360°— make it 340° or 380° so he is not always facing exactly where he was before.) The last stage of this phase it to move the dog around the box to face a different side before sending him.

As he gets reliable at finding the right article, you can introduce more and more articles into the box until there are twenty or more articles (that's why the box was 4' by 4' from the start!) You can use anything that the dog can retrieve. In my own box there are over one hundred articles, including: old dumbbells, broken dumbbells, iron bolts, skate wheels, old shoes, a mop head, used plastic shower gel containers, metal clips, bits of leather, old tooth brushes, broken tools (not sharp ones!), rubber luggage straps, a jug kettle, and so on. Use anything that is not dangerous!

For the next step, you will have to use a different article from the box each day. Leave all the previously used articles in the box. Now you are teaching the dog to retrieve the article with your **strongest** scent on it.

Advanced Scent Discrimination

Your Different Scent Locations

You will have noticed that I frequently refer to 'holding the article in your hand' and giving the dog scent 'with your hand'. This is because different 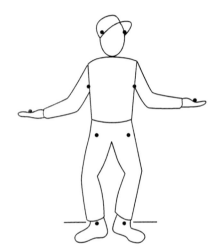 parts of your body have varying odors. Oh yes, they all bear YOUR SCENT, but each part of your body varies slightly from others.

Provided your dog is already good at scent discrimination, you can prove this for yourself and have some fun while doing so. As a bonus, the exercise will sharpen your dog's nasal abilities.

Discriminating Between Body Parts

Take ten clean handkerchiefs that were all washed, rinsed, and dried together so that they start off smelling exactly the same. Put two next to your feet (one inside each sock), put two inside your underwear, two under a hat, one under each armpit, and hold the remaining two in your hands. Leave the cloths in place about a half an hour... long enough for you to have enough scent on the cloths to carry out this delicate experiment.

Now put one of each pair in a line along the floor about fifteen inches apart. Give the dog the scent of the other 'hand cloth' and send him to do scent in your normal way. Be patient. As mentioned, this is quite a delicate operation and your dog may not realize straight away that the cloths do, in fact, smell different. Remember—the dog is used to searching for individual human scent... now we are asking him to break this down even further. With ordinary scent discrimination, I advise only to give scent for three seconds — and not stifle the dog while doing so! However, for this task, give the dog scent for about twice as long (six seconds is good), but still hold the cloth at least an inch or so from his nose.

Practice with only your 'hand scent' until the dog is proficient. Once he is reliable at that, try one of the other cloths.

You MUST thoroughly wash the cloths again each time before using a cloth from a different part of the body! When giving him this new scent, hold the cloth only by one corner and make sure your other hand is not behind it (or touches it in any way). We don't want the dog to cue in to your hand scent if you are working on the scent from say, under your arms.

If ever your dog makes a mistake (and thus contaminates a cloth), the cloths must all be washed again. Store each pair separately if you are going to continue with the same cloths for any length of time. It will be easier for you if you make a large number of sterile cloths up in the beginning.

Once your dog is reliable with you putting out just the five cloths, then you can put out all nine cloths (apart from the one you are giving the dog scent from).

Remember: if you get any of the cloths contaminated with scent from another cloth, the dog will soon become confused and may give up trying forever!

Scent Discrimination: Your Scent vs. Another Person's

At this point, you are ready to train your dog to distinguish between your scent and the scent of other people. To do this, you will need the assistance of friends.

Firstly, take an article out of the box and have a friend lightly touch all the articles remaining in the box. Throw your article back into the box and send the dog as before. The first time you do this, the dog may be a little unsure... just be patient. He will realize that it is the article (with the scent he has been given) that is the one you want him to bring back.

Gradually, through time, let your friend (or friends, if you have more than one!!!) touch the articles for longer periods of time—depositing more of their scent. Eventually, ask them to hold the articles in their hands, and finally have them hold them as long as you hold your article to intensify the scent. If you give your scent to the dog, he will bring back the article you handled from among the articles bearing other people's scent. 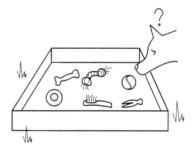 This is actually easier for the dog than finding your 'hot' scent from other articles bearing your (weaker) scent.

Your dog is very capable of doing this, and even more. All we have to do is let the dog know what is required of him—which is the hardest part of any exercise.

To expand the dog's repertoire, start him retrieving articles bearing other people's scent. To do this, leave all the articles in the box untouched for a few days. Then, get a friend to take an article out of the box, handle it and throw it back. Instruct your friend to hold his hand in front of the dog's nose briefly, and send the dog after the article. He may not be accurate the first time, but will soon realize what is wanted. Remember, NEVER tell your dog off if he makes a mistake! Be patient, and he will soon reward you.

Over a period of time, you will be able to handle the other items in the box more and more and even get other people to do so. Give the dog the scent of a person who has handled only one article. The greatest advance is to have several people handle various articles and your dog can distinguish one person's scent from among many. You can get plenty of practice in with everyone who comes to your house... this will not only impress visitors, it will give your dog plenty of variety. Very quickly, your dog will be able to accurately identify objects that have only been held for a second, honestly!

All dogs are capable of every form of Nosework...

Searching for Articles

Searching for hidden articles is an entirely different application than sorting out one by its scent. With scent, the articles are all obvious to the dog and he is given a specific scent which tells him which article you want brought back to you.

In searching, the articles are not in obvious view and the dog is not given a specific scent. The dog is taught to bring back **anything** bearing human scent. (In competitions there is a further distinction: in scent, the handler is in the ring with the dog and the articles; in searching, the handler is outside the marked square in which the dog is working.)

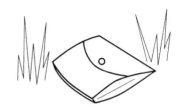

The practical application of searching is that the dog can locate any item that his owner (or another person) has lost. When I was in the Police, my dog not only found many things concerned with crime, but was able to assist law abiding citizens as well. One time I was approached by a worried looking man who had mislaid his car keys in a clearing in Epping Forest where he had gone with his secretary to catch up on some office work (!). He was due home to his loving wife shortly and could not find the car's ignition keys. Within two minutes, my dog had brought back the keys and the man was very grateful (!).

When I was a Constable, the Dog Sergeant was asked to find an engagement ring lost by a young lady. She had left the cinema with her fiancé and had dislodged the ring when she pulled off her gloves. After the crowds leaving the cinema had dispersed, the Sergeant instructed his dog and within a few minutes the dog had found the ring lodged upright against the curb.

My wife once lost her St. Christopher chain at a yoga class outside somewhere on a school field. She was very vague as to where she had been when she shook out her blanket thus losing the emblem. I took my dog back to the school where I had about a half acre to search. In less than ten minutes, wife and St. Christopher were reunited.

The reason I have given 'non-criminal' examples is so that you can see how useful this exercise can be. It's fun and well worth the exercise of developing your dog's natural capabilities in case you ever need to make use of it. Maybe one day a person will approach you saying that a wallet containing $5,000 has been lost. If your dog finds it and you get a ten percent reward, you'll be very pleased with yourself and your dog. If this ever happens, remember who inspired you!

Training the Article Search

Play with your dog with his favorite toy. Let him bring it back to you a few times (not formal retrieves). We do not want formality in training for this. Now throw the toy in some long grass and let him go after it straight away. (See Diagram.) No command is necessary at this early stage of training.

Wind

Repeat the above, but this time hold the dog back physically for a few seconds before releasing him to go after the toy. DO NOT command the dog to SIT before sending him—he may break, and then what are you going to do? If you 'tell him off', he may be put off from going after the thrown article. If you don't tell him off, he has gotten away with disobeying a command (Sit).

Note: on a still day, it doesn't matter in which direction you throw the toy. On a windy day the toy should be thrown into the wind so that the scent of the article is being blown towards the dog (the opposite of the initial technique discussed in the tracking section.)

When the dog has brought the article back a few times reliably and happily, you can introduce your command. I use PICK IT UP for any exercise where the dog leaves my side and comes back with something in his mouth. If I require a 'formal present' (or a 'front') I use the word FETCH. I realize that fetch is a hard sounding word and I advise my students to use something kinder (like HOLD) even though I am too old to change myself!

After a couple of successful repetitions of the "toy thrown in the tall grass", you are now ready to get the dog to use his nose. Up to this time the dog has seen **where** you threw the article each time.

Tease the dog with the toy, throw it into the long grass while keeping him held back. Now, instead of sending him directly, turn him around in a 360° circle and send him—using your command. The dog will probably go straight to the article again. The purpose of this is to get the dog used to being turned before being sent.

Repeat the above exercise, but this time don't turn exactly 360°—turn either more or less than 360°—so that the dog is not facing directly in the direction where the toy was thrown. When the dog is proficient at this exercise, then you can walk the dog away from the area and bring him back before sending him. You can also start to send the dog from different points.

The final step is to leave the dog in his kennel (or the car) while you place the toy out in the grass. Take the dog near to and downwind from the toy and send him in. At first, praise the dog when he gets near the article. Gradually cut of this praise and allow the dog to become more self reliant.

Note: if the dog searches unsuccessfully for too long he will become discouraged. If you notice this behavior, surreptitiously drop another article near him so that he can find that one and have a success. Make a big fuss over the find and end that session right there. A dog must ALWAYS have a success to keep motivated to repeat this exercise.

If you are searching in a practical situation and the dog comes up with nothing, then drop the article as described so that the dog is successful. The dog **must** find something every time you send him—he **must** have faith in you. Any failure is likely to lessen his enthusiasm next time. Too many failures will stop the dog from working at all!!! Some dogs need the handler to keep encouraging them verbally while they are working and some dogs become distracted by the constant talk. Experiment with your dog to determine what suits him best. You must learn how to work your own dog!

Searching for Large (Irretrievable) Articles

Large articles that a dog cannot retrieve are treated like finding a person. The dog is taught to bark at them (see the appendix for training your dog to alert with barking).

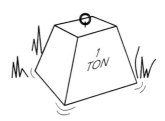

Imagine that you have sent your dog into some woods to find articles bearing human scent. He finds a bicycle. "I can't ride this!" says he. So, he barks to get his handler (who can ride it) to come and assist him. He finds a safe. "Too heavy," he thinks. Again, he gets his handler to come and help.

Another type or irretrievable article is something the dog could normally carry, but is out of reach or fixed to something. Again, the dog whistles up assistance.

Some dogs do this naturally. You throw a ball (toy) and it accidentally lands in a tree. After a while of poncing around the base of the tree, the dog starts to bark in frustration. You get the ball out of the tree and give it to the

dog. The dog has learned, "I bark, he acts." Who is training whom? As I said before, a dog will repeat an action that he finds rewarding. The more rewarding the incident, the less the number of repetitions it takes for the dog to learn. In this circumstance, one repetition is probably enough.

To train for irretrievable articles, either place or throw out something in the presence of the dog that is either too heavy, too large or awkward for the dog to pick up. Make sure it has an abundance of your scent on it.

Holding the dog back by the collar, "gee him up" (get him excited), give your command and release him. He will rush up to the item and try to pick it up. Keep encouraging him. He may start to scratch or paw at it. (Allow him to do this for now.) If he doesn't eventually speak, command him to do so. When he speaks, rush up to him full of praise and excitement. Throw a ball or toy for him as a reward.

Repeat this several times with the same article in different locations. Then repeat it with different articles in the same locations. (Otherwise the dog begins to think he can only bark at this item in this location.) Now try putting the same items and some new items up in trees, on ledges, in the shrubbery— all out of reach of the dog. Both person and dog will find this FUN!!!

Make a mixture of articles: some the dog can retrieve, some the dog cannot. Again, FUN!

Hunt the Thimble

Just as we can utilize our dog to search for articles outside, we can also do the same indoors. This exercise can be practical (from a Police point of view) in a building search, or entertainment in our own homes.

Step one: start off with a toy the dog really likes. Let someone hold the dog back rather than giving the dog a demotivatory 'sit-stay'. Tease the dog with the toy, and let him see you put it partially under the corner of a rug or cushion. Go back to the dog and get him really excited—release him with an excitable informal command (see the appendix on retrieving). He will immediately get the toy for you. At this time the dog is using his eyes rather than his nose, but we will soon fix that.

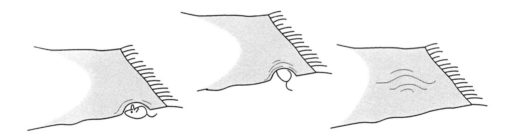

Repeat this exercise (still in full sight) by putting the toy further and further under the rug or cushion until finally the toy cannot be seen.

Step Two: go back to the very beginning and start all over—in a different place. When the dog is proficient in both places, introduce another place the same way.

Step Three: let the dog see you place the article in the first location you used. Take the dog out of the room, and move the toy to the second position.

Bring the dog back in the room and get him really excited. Send him for the toy with your informal command. When the dog discovers for himself that the toy is not in the first place where he saw you put it, he may work it out for himself and go to the second position. If he doesn't, then you must encourage him towards it. When he get near it, encourage him. **Only encourage him this first time!** Ever after this, let him work it out and reserve your praise until he is on his way back to you with the toy in his mouth.

Step Four: repeat the above using any of the three places familiar to the dog. Take the dog out of the room and switch the toy to one of the other two spots.

Step Five: start using different places—still out of sight—but initially near to the original ones. When you see that the dog knows what the 'game' is, you can put the toy anywhere in the room and eventually, anywhere in the house.

Step Six: The only thing left is to start using different articles. Begin with other toys at first until the dog will search for anything bearing your recent scent. You can also use scent from other people providing that you have 'given scent' to the dog before sending him.

This game is called Hunt the Thimble in England. You may know of it by a different name! When this game is played with children, the youngster is encouraged not only by what we say ("You are getting warmer, colder" or "You are burning" when close to the item...) but also by the tone of our voice and the excitement (or lack of it) we put in it. It is the same for training a dog. You can use the same words if you like, but let your voice convey the message!

An Englishwoman with a Miniature Schnauzer named Sparky used to do just that in the Area Search (Search for Articles) in our Working Trials. As she approached the search square, she could be heard saying "We're going to play Hunt the Thimble, Sparky!" much to the amusement of all the macho Police Officers also competing. When she started saying, "You're getting warmer!" (if she had seen the article), they rolled about laughing. They laughed on the other side of their faces when Sparky brought in ALL four articles in two minutes when they had only gotten two in the full time allowed of five minutes...

This game can amuse your children or grandchildren. You never know when you will need it in a practical situation. Now, just where have I left that darned cordless telephone?

Searching for People (Hide and Seek)

Searching for people is the same as searching for articles, but on a much larger scale! Practical applications of this exercise are used by the Police Departments to find criminals hiding in buildings and in areas where tracking is inappropriate (no starting point) and for Search and Rescue handlers to find lost or missing persons. Police also find lost people: children who have gone astray, old people who have wandered off and mentally incapacitated persons—people who might be in serious danger if left unprotected or out all night. Search and Rescue groups are called in when disaster strikes: avalanches, earthquakes, hikers lost in the mountains, etc. Finding hidden persons is also a requirement of some competitions.

What we are aiming at here is to follow the same basic principles as playing 'hide and seek' where a person is 'it' and the dog is the seeker.

As I said, it is the same as looking for articles and the training is the same—including wind direction. You must get the dog interested in the person (we'll call him or her the helper) just as you got the dog interested in the article. You can do this by asking the helper to throw an article for the dog several times. If possible, get the dog to 'speak' at the helper to throw the ball (helpful later on when you want the dog to bark as the signal to you that a person has been found). Initially you will command the dog to bark, later the helper will get the dog to bark. When the dog is speaking readily, go on to the next step.

Now, take your helper and throw him into some very tall grass!!! (See Diagram.) Or, if the helper is too heavy or large, then instruct him to go and hide behind a bush.

Wind

The handler holds the dog's collar. The helper teases the dog with the article, and instead of throwing it, the handler runs away from the dog and

disappears behind a bush. The handler releases the dog as soon as the helper disappears. The dog will naturally rush out and find the helper who throws the

article for the dog as soon as he has been 'found'. The handler calls the dog back to himself, takes the article from the dog and hands it back to the helper who now has rejoined the handler.

Repeat the last exercise, but this time the helper delays throwing the article until the dog has barked—then it is immediately thrown for the dog. Again, the handler calls the dog back to himself, takes the ball from the dog and hands it to the helper. Repeat this until the dog realizes what is required and is happily doing it. Then, you can introduce your command. (Personally I use FIND HIM!)

Just as was done with searching for articles, the dog is eventually turned through circles of varying degrees. Then the dog is moved to a different spot before being sent.

And, remember, it will also be easier and faster for the dog to find the person if you make use of the wind direction—the wind needs to be blowing *from the hidden person towards the dog*. If a dog is slow at 'catching on', he can be held by a third party while the handler runs and hides. (After two or three repetitions, the handler holds the dog while the helper runs and hides.)

Now that the dog is competent at going to one location, it is time to introduce a second. Send the dog to find the helper (and be rewarded with an article) until the dog is adept at the new place too.

Here's the exciting bit! The handler holds the dog so that the dog is able to see the helper run away and disappear in one of the spots that has been

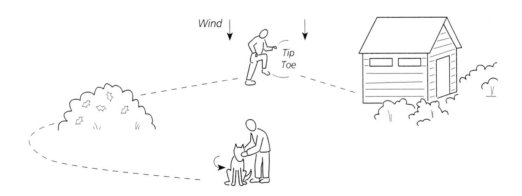

used up until now. The handler turns the dog away and the helper then runs in a roundabout way to the other spot (See Diagram.) The dog is turned to face the place where he saw the handler disappear (spot #1), is commanded to find the person and released. The dog will run to spot #1 because he saw the helper go there.

When the dog discovers that the helper is not there, he will probably look towards his handler. (If he doesn't the handler must get his attention.) The handler indicates the other position (spot #2) by using hand, arm and/or body movements to entice the dog to go there. When the dog finds the helper at spot #2, he is rewarded by having the article thrown. After a couple of repetitions, the dog will automatically go to the second or alternative location when he finds the first empty.

WARNING: do not always leave the first place vacant. The dog must be taught to thoroughly investigate each place he visits. If we leave the first one unoccupied frequently, the dog learns to make only a cursory search of the first one or ignores the first one altogether.

The next step in the game is for the dog to be commanded to search without the prior motivation of seeing the helper run away. The helper is now in place BEFORE the dog is brought to the scene. (See Diagram.) To make it easier for the dog, the handler directs the dog to the correct spot the first time.

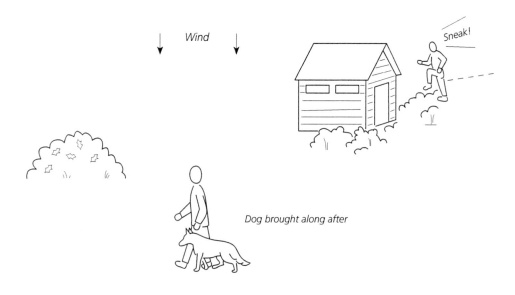

It is time to introduce a third site (spot #3). Once the dog is familiar with this one, you can use all three. Sometimes the helper will be hiding in the first spot to be explored, sometimes hiding in the second or third. Many people lose points in competitions because they have allowed the habit of being casual in the approach to the first few hides. Obviously, careful searching is even more important for Police or Search and Rescue dogs. If they miss someone, the results could be serious.

Once the dog is searching accurately in the familiar places, it is time to move on into unfamiliar territory. The helper hides first. The dog is brought to the location, commanded and released. (See Diagram.) It is IMPERATIVE that the dog always finds someone, and finds them reasonably quickly in the initial training stages. If the dog appears to be in difficulty or losing interest in the search, the helper must make a noise or rustle the bushes to attract the

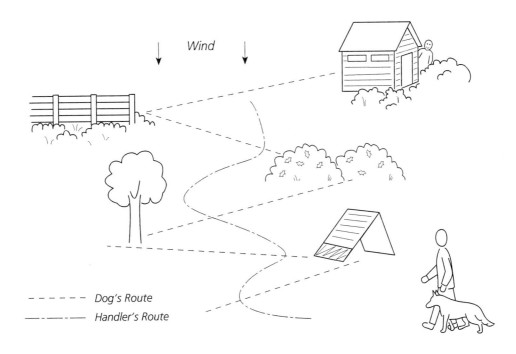

dog. Be careful not to do it too often or the dog will become lazy and rely on it. Make sure that the wind is in the correct direction.

Remember: the dog must always end up with a success! If you are ever using this "game" in a practical situation and the dog doesn't find someone, then a person must volunteer to hide in an easy place so that the dog will finish with a success.

Once your dog is quartering the ground enthusiastically, locating the person accurately, and speaking readily, we can make the game Hide-and-Seek even more fun.

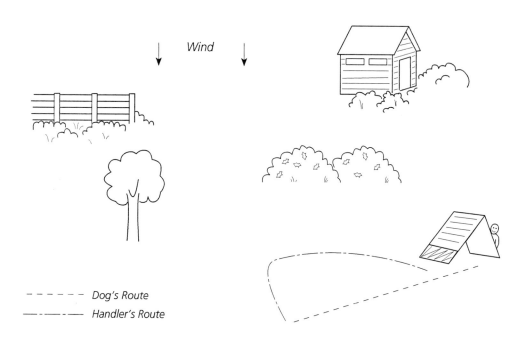

– – – – – – Dog's Route

—–—·–— Handler's Route

Remember—to ensure that the dog always covers the whole of the area, occasionally put the helper in the nearest hiding place to the dog. We don't want the dog to skip any areas! (See Diagram.)

The helper can occasionally hide up a tree. Note that I said occasionally! If you do this too often, your dog will run around just looking up trees.

You can now get the helper to hide in more difficult places. Use places where the helper will be completely out of sight—even when the dog is right with him! The dog will be working on scent alone. You are limited only by your imagination...

Another way of advancing this exercise is to enlarge the area to be searched before finding anyone. In Scotland, the Search and Rescue Dogs are expected to work well away from their handlers and to search an area of up to one-quarter of a mile square.

I was once buried for a dog to find in a huge area on the side of a mountain. The "grave" (as it is ominously called) was six feet deep. As the Instructor put the last shovelful over me, he said, "The dog will find you in half an hour." Sure enough, at exactly half an hour later, I heard the excited sniffing and panting of a dog.

The next minute, I heard the handler calling his dog away. "Just like some Police Dog Handlers!" thought I. After a while I started to get concerned. "What if there's a white-out?" "What if the person who buried me breaks a leg?" "What if everyone is called off on a full scale emergency and they forget me!!" "What if..."

Exactly another half an hour later I heard the sniffing and grunting of a dog. What a relief. Then the sound of digging, and eventually two paws followed by the beautiful face of a yellow Labrador (this was one of the top working dogs who was capable of working a quarter mile square). Oh what joy!!! I'll tell you, it was an experience... it was nice to get back to the Hotel and have some hot toddy!

There is no reason you cannot try this when there is a heavy fall of snow. First, get someone to hold your dog. Get the dog excited and run thirty yards away from him. Jump into a "grave" that has been previously dug out. (See Diagram.) Shout your dog's name excitedly. Your helper releases the dog and he rushes out to find you. Praise!

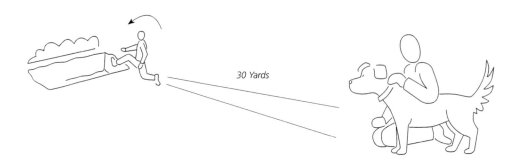

30 Yards

Next time, run out, jump in the grave and get a third helper to cover you with a sprinkling of snow. Have the dog released. He will find you by location and scent. Gradually increase the depth to which you are covered (buried). OR, increase the distance the dog is held away from the grave. When your dog has been finding and indicating you readily every time, he can be moved further away from the spot he has been occupying before he is sent. ***Remember, DO NOT increase two things at the same time! It will confuse the dog and he will lose confidence in himself AND in you.***

Now you can also begin to turn the dog in partial circles (review the section on scent discrimination) to disorient him. Now the dog will have to locate you... and once the covering of snow over you is level with the snow on the ground, he will locate you purely by nosework.

Finally, have a third party bury you without the dog being present. Your helper brings the dog out to the area and releases him to find you. Expand this training the same way done in the earlier section by sending him for a helper. Remember the praise and/or article toss for a reward!

Searching Large Areas

When the dog is working well in unfamiliar places, then it is time to start searching larger areas. Get a friend to hide in an area where there are plenty of hiding places.

In the open (if possible) work your dog in zigzag lines across the area and into the wind. (See Diagram page 35.) At first you will need to walk in a slight zigzag yourself to guide the dog. Later you will be able to walk straight up the center of a field and direct your dog to either side. Insist that the dog investigate any places a helper could hide. As soon as the dog indicates that he has found someone, really encourage him. He will first "tell you" that he has found a person by the sudden movement of his head and change in direction. Move up behind him, and when he has barked readily for some time, get the helper to throw the article.

The reason we use an article (such as a ball) and get the helper to throw it in searching for people is because we want to prevent aggression from creeping in. Even Police dogs are searching for innocent people more often then they are for villains. It's no good going back to the mother of a lost child and saying "Here's her arm. We will bring back the rest of her later!" It's no good finding a person with a broken leg at the bottom of a gully and the dog creating more wounds than the victim already has! Keep the atmosphere light and playful. Do not urge the dog on—let the pleasure and the motivation come from the person being found.

Building Searches

Buildings can (and should) be used as well as open places although building searches are a different discipline. While the dog's olfactory sense is still the main way of finding a hidden person, there are other things to be considered.

The effect of air currents become even more important inside because they need more interpretation. The hidden person may be very hard to locate, even though the dog is indicating clearly by barking at a certain spot. (See Diagram.)

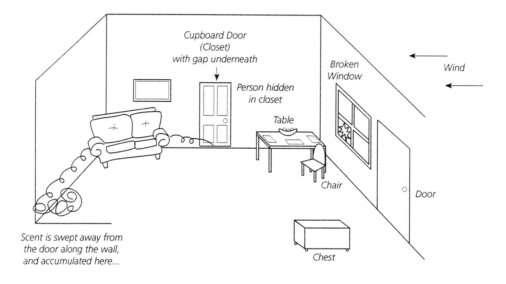

The handler must work more closely with his dog—becoming an even stronger team. The dog barks to say "there is someone here!" and the handler has to work out the exact location in many cases.

Various things may affect the air currents and thus the location of where the scent of the person is the strongest. A partly open (or broken) window, an air vent, underground passages with cracks in the floor, broken tiles on the roof, big gaps in the eaves—all these things may affect the movement of air currents to different degrees according to the strength and direction of the 'wind'. Here we are talking about whole buildings. How much more will the air circulate in damaged, derelict or collapsed structures?

In hotter weather, the air—being thinner—will circulate faster than when it is colder (thicker). Warm air is also 'lighter' than cold air and will tend to move upwards while cold air sinks. (See Diagram.)

We must be very systematic when going about a building search. It is easy to miss areas or complete rooms if we are haphazard. AND, a person can move either from an unsearched area to a searched area, or right out of the building altogether! You might be thinking that this applies only to Police Dogs looking for criminals, but a lost person may become disoriented or the person being sought may be mentally impaired. One person (with or without a dog) should remain outside a building to see if anyone leaves.

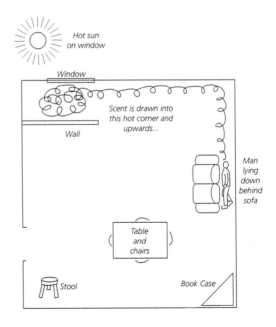

If there is a person on the outside to safeguard the surroundings, then, one way of proceeding is for the search team to go straight to the top of the building and work downwards—clearing every room on each floor before descending to the floor below. If the person being sought hears a dog above him and keeps going down, he will eventually go outside to be spotted by the person left outside.

The dog should remain in eyesight of his handler who reads the smallest of indications (behaviors) from the dog. (Your dog may bark only when he is absolutely sure of himself.) In dangerous situations (an unsafe building for example), television cameras have been strapped to the backs of dogs while the handler stays back. For fun, you could try it with a video camera and get a dog's eye view!

Derelict sites can be used as well as new construction. Make sure things are SAFE for both humans and dogs as well as having permission to use such areas.

Searching small rooms can be left to the dog, but larger rooms or warehouses need a handler to decide how to cover the area systematically—either from the perimeter in, or from the center out like the spokes of a wheel. Personally, I always allowed my dog to do his own thing first. If that yielded no results or if I thought some of the area was missed, then I would guide my dog with voice or hand signals.

Some 'villains' tend to always hide off the ground—thinking that a dog couldn't find them. (James Cagney always did in films!) They do not realize that they are making a dog's job easier. Scent falls downwards in time, and the longer they are hidden, the more concentration of scent accumulating below them. (See Diagram.) So, handlers, look up!

I was once called to a huge warehouse many miles from my own "patch" because there was thought to be a "suspect on the premises". On arriving, I found twelve members of the local "gendarmerie" departing. "We have searched it all," they called. "There is no one in there." Since I had come a long way at high speed, I told them that I would nevertheless put the dog in. The locals thought I was wasting my time (and the time of the Bobby who would have to remain.) I put my Rottweiler in one door and within seconds, he was barking. The locals came rushing back before they even had time to get in their vehicles.

The villain had climbed up onto the wooden beams when he heard the Police arrive. When the officers entered, they turned on powerful search lights. Even if one of them had looked up (not many do) they would not have seen the guy although he was in clear view. The sense of sight was useless in this instance, but the sense of smell was important. All the time the person sat high up on the beam, his scent was descending. If the scent pool could have been seen, it must have formed a big puddle below him. The strength of his scent was intensified by the fear developed when I followed the usual routine of shouting, "Come on out! Police Dog coming in two minutes!" I then would cue Abelard to bark. (It was more like a roar!) The pool of scent would then be doubled!!! Sometimes villains would come out of buildings before I could put Abelard in... the sound of his bark put shivers in their spines...

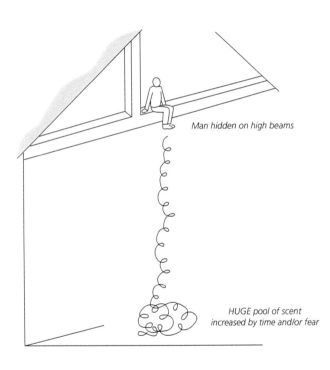

Man hidden on high beams

HUGE pool of scent increased by time and/or fear

Kitchen Cupboard Fun

Scenting Essences

You probably have various essences (for cooking or baking) in your kitchen cabinets right now. You can use these essences to do a variation on scent work with your dog. Any use of the dog's olfactory organs will help develop the dog's ability to use scent for any other reason. It is also FUN!

Start with a strong essence or flavoring such as peppermint. (Pure oils are too strong—use the flavorings for cooking/baking which are already partly diluted.) Fill a dish washing bowl with water. Take eight pieces of paper towels from a roll and dip six of them in the plain water—wringing each one out and placing them in a line on the floor. Now put one drop of peppermint essence in the water. (See Diagram.)

Dip the last two paper towels in the peppermint water and wring them out. Place one of them at the end of the line of towels on the floor (you may find that your dog works better if you screw or twist the papers up). Give the dog the scent from the other towel (see Diagram) and tell him to fetch.

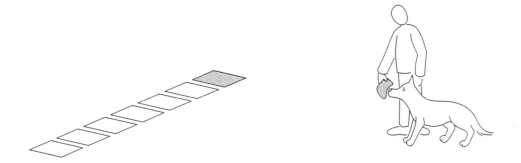

Many dogs will search along the line and bring back the correct one right away. If your dog brings back the wrong one, do not chastise him in any way. Gently take it from him, give the dog the scent and send him again. Repeat until he picks up the right one and then go to town with your praise!

Once he has got the correct one and has been praised and rewarded, finish for the day. Repeat this procedure exactly the same way the next day with new towels. He will probably 'work the towels' with his nose and pick up the correct one straight away.

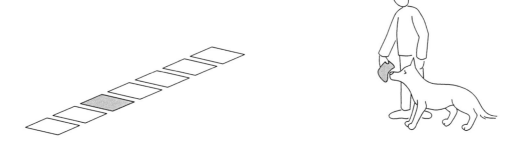

Do not praise him while he is sniffing the right one—wait until he returns to you with it. You do not want him to rely on you for help. Once he has gotten the right one, move one of the plain water towels out of the line with your foot (do not contaminate it with your peppermint hands!) to create a space. Drop one of the peppermint towels in the space, give the dog the scent with the other and send him again.

On day three, wring out six new towels in plain water. Place them on the ground in a line with a space between any two. Add one drop of peppermint essence to the bowl of water. Now pour half of the scented water away and refill the bowl with plain water. Dip and wring out two new tissues. Place one in the space you created, and give the dog the scent of the second one. Send the dog, etc...

Continue this exercise daily—each day pour out half of the bowl, fill it back up with plain, pour out half again and fill it with plain again... etc. (Each day the mixture will be diluted twice as much as the previous day.) I had a dog that could distinguish between plain water cloths and a cloth that had been dipped in a forty gallon rain barrel that had one drop of peppermint flavoring added. Peppermint smuggling has never been a problem here in Great Britain, so the Customs and Excise Authorities never required a peppermint finding dog!

Repeat this exercise from the beginning with other items from your cupboard: vanilla, almond, orange... you can also use coffee from your morning cup! Vinegar has a distinctive smell. So does peanut butter! (This could get messy and the dog might be tempted to eat the cloths.) You can experiment as much as you like!

If you hooked on this game, you can use handkerchiefs or squares of cloth instead of paper towels. ***Great care must be taken not to contaminate any cloths with the wrong scent.*** This training is very delicate. It is NOT the same for the dog as identifying animal or human scents. It will not take much to confuse your dog and stop him from trying. Be patient and take your time with each step and you will be rewarded with your dog's educated nose.

Distinguishing Between Essences

The next stage is to distinguish between a number of non-human scents. Up to this point, you have been encouraging your dog to bring back one distinctive smell from among neutral smells. You can still use paper towels if you wish, but instead of using plain water for the 'undesired' towels, use very dilute solutions of a different essence. For the towel that you want the dog to retrieve, go back to using a very strong solution (one drop in the full bowl). Over a period of time, get the two proportions nearer together in strength. Either make the decoy one gradually stronger OR the required one made gradually weaker. NEVER do the two alterations at the same time.

Once the dog can distinguish between two towels equal in the strength of their different scents, then you can add others until all of your towels are different.

Discriminating Between Hot and Cold Water Taps

Wring few cloths out which have been wetted from the cold water tap or faucet in your kitchen and lay them out on the floor. Now, wring out two cloths under the hot water tap. (The water need not be hot at the time, but if it is, you can put the test off until the cloths are cold—but it is not necessary.)

Lay one 'hot water tap' cloth among the 'cold' cloths. Use the second hot water cloth to give the dog the scent. Send the dog to find the hot water cloth. It works! Even with 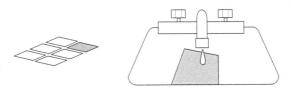 modern plumbing running through plastic pipes, the chemical changes that take place by having hot water run through one system will probably be enough for the dog to mark the difference.

Demonstrating Your Dog's Abilities

Playing Cards

In the USA, the American Kennel Club competition for the Utility Dog title requires that the dog pick out the handler's 'hottest' scented article from a group of the same articles (leather and metal). All the articles have the latent scent of the handler on them, and also the scent of the Steward who placed them on the ground approximately six inches apart from one another. Cloths used in British competitions are placed two feet apart.

The method of training I use for scent work does not specify distance that items have to be apart. Instead of limiting the number of items being searched, I have made no bounds. My scent box contains at least one hundred articles.

With a pack of cards, I use all 52... plus the two jokers! They are not placed two feet apart, nor six inches. They are, in some cases, actually touching. (See Diagram.)

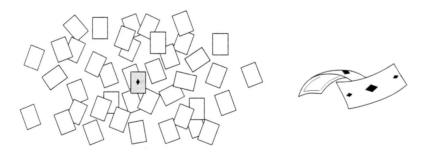

When I demonstrate this with my own dog Tim, I get someone to take a card from the pack (an old, well handled pack), and curve the card over their left forearm while using the palm of their right hand to keep the card in place.

I deal the remaining fifty-three cards onto the floor. The cards stay where they land—some two or three inches apart, some overlapping. The person is then asked to place the extra card anywhere in a space among the other cards and to give Tim his or her scent. (This is done by the person holding their open hand an inch from Tim's nose for two or three seconds.)

Tim is then sent to "PICK IT UP". Most of the time he does this straight away after investigating the cards on the floor. But sometimes (if he is unsuccessful for too long) he panics and starts picking up any old card. He is then calmed down, the card re-scented and he is given scent again. He then goes out and picks the correct card after searching.

By the way—all the cards have been curved slightly so that he can pick them up easily from the flat floor. If only one card was curved (over the helpers arm) then it could be said that Tim recognized it by sight rather than scent. This probably would not be the case, but why gives skeptics occasion to doubt Tim's nose.

Training to Play with Cards

Training for this is rather easy. First, train the dog on your own scent. Take a few cards out of the pack, curve them over your arm and scatter them on the floor a few inches apart to start with. (I don't say 'bend' them because it might be interpreted as folding them sharply.)

Pick one of the cards up and rub it between your hands. Place it on the floor among the others. Give your dog your scent (briefly) and send him to pick it up. When he does so, lavish rewards on him. If you have worked your way through this book, I believe your dog will be successful the very first time.

You can now rapidly increase the number of cards on the floor until you are using the whole pack. When the dog is proficient with your own scent in a full pack, introduce other people to scent one card for the dog to find.

To proceed even further with playing cards, we need to teach the dog to play blackjack. Sorry! Just my little joke! What we actually do is teach the dog to pick a card that has been handled by one person from the rest of the pack which has been handled by another person.

To start training this, get another person to 'deal' all the cards instead of doing the task yourself. This gets your dog used to other people's scent as 'decoys' instead of your own. Send the dog after a card you have handled by giving him your scent. When he is successful, go on to the next step.

If, at any time, the dog goes wrong, do not make a big deal about it. Take the wrong card from him—showing no emotion. Re-scent the correct card, and give the dog the scent again. He will learn more quickly if he is not stressed.

Now, get the other person to deal half the pack while you deal the other half. A third person will handle and place the required card among those on the floor. The third party gives the scent to the dog and the dog retrieves that card.

Next, get the third party to just touch five or six cards while you deal the rest. The person handling the required card puts plenty of scent on it. Give scent and send the dog.

Finally, you can get several people to briefly handle some of the cards. When your dog is capable of finding the correct card—discriminating the correct scent from several different (weaker) ones, you can have 'decoy' people put more and more scent on their cards.

You are now in a position to show off your dog at parties, demonstrations, and in classes!

Playing with Dominoes

Another game to amaze your friends, co-workers, or at school demonstrations is to do scent discrimination with dominoes... a good use for a set with a few pieces missing!

Hold the open box of dominoes about three feet from the floor and tip all the pieces out. This height will ensure that the dominoes spread out a little, but not too much. (You may need to experiment at home to find out the best height for your own set in their own particular box.) Whatever way the dominoes land, leave them as they are.

Ask someone to pick up a domino at random and examine it carefully. (It can be either one that landed face up or face down... it doesn't matter.) The chosen domino is then passed to you. Hold it in your hand for a few seconds while you pretend to be looking intently at the dots. Tell your audience that you are using ESP to tell your dog which domino has been chosen.

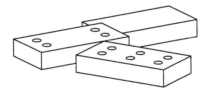

Having held it long enough, place it FACE DOWN anywhere among the other dominoes, being careful not to touch any of the rest. Continue with your thought transference and tell your dog the name of the domino you want him to bring to you. As you use a signal to send him out, you can surreptitiously give him scent with your hand. The person who chose the domino will have put his or her scent on it as well when handling it, and a slight amount of this will have been transferred to your hand.

If you have done enough training to get your dog competent at scent, then the dog should bring the right one back. With a flourish you show the face of the domino to the assembled crowd!

If your dog happens to have an "off day" and can't find it, or brings back the wrong one, you can say that your mental communication has broken down, so you will have to put the domino face up and TELL him which one is wanted. Ask for a volunteer to hold the dog facing away from the dominos so that the dog doesn't 'cheat' by watching where you put it. As you pick it up, have another good look at it (while reinforcing your ESP. (This will be an excuse to hold the domino longer.) Then replace the domino in the same position. This time when you send your dog, tell him to bring back the double two — or whatever the chosen one was.

If you have done your groundwork with scent discrimination, then there should be no need to fall back on excuses. Practice in different locations by yourself, and then with one or two friends present until the dog is infallible before 'going public' with your demonstration.

You can work out the most impressive way to present your dog to the best advantage by trying as many variations you can think of using dominos in this way.

How to Use "Choice" to Your Advantage

Conjurers know many ways to get an audience to make the choice of the item they want them to. One of these methods is to write all the items on a black board (or flip chart) in rows and columns.

Ask the audience if they want the top half, or the bottom half. If they say they want the top half and this contains the item you want, then you just erase the bottom half. If your item is in the lower half, then you say, "Okay! You want the top, then that leaves the bottom half for me!" Then erase the top half.

Next, ask them if they want the left column of the right. Repeat as above, leaving the half containing your item.

Continue until there is only one item left... that will be the very one that you have in mind and that you have been holding in your hand all the while the audience's 'choice' has been going on. (This will make sure your scent on the item is strong.)

Ball Glove Hat	Belt Sock Keys
Paper Pen Diskette	**Toy Shoe Scarf**

If you are using dominos, you could (for example) choose the double blank as the one the dog will retrieve. Keep all the other dominos in the box. When the audience has 'voluntarily' chosen the double blank, tip out all the dominos onto the floor, dropping the one you have been holding with them. Spread them out with minimal contact and send your dog in!

Sometimes there will be a smart mouth in the audience who will realize that you are 'forcing a choice'. He will say, "First time you erased the half we chose, and the second time the reverse." Don't get cross or enter a debate... just tell the audience that you are in their hands and they are making the choices, then quickly move on.

An alternate method is to have the audience shout out their choices all together, then you can be selective in interpretation in what was shouted out. Quite often they choose the one you want anyway!

You can use this process of 'forcing a choice' with dominos, playing cards, or chess pieces... indeed, you can use just about anything.

Chess Pieces (No knowledge of chess is necessary)

Carry the Black King in your pocket for a few days, handling it frequently. If possible, wash all the other pieces in unscented soap, rinse them thoroughly, and leave in the open air to dry. Put them carefully back into the box and do not handle them again.

When you want to show off your dog, place the chess board on the floor. Ask for a volunteer to place all the pieces on the board for you. (It is always good to involve members of the audience.) Pass him or her the box — which now contains the Black King which has been put back at one end on the top at the very last minute. Although the volunteer will handle the Black King and contaminate it, this will still be the only piece with a strong amount of your own scent on it. Make sure you give the dog scent WITH YOUR HAND as you send him out to the chess board to bring you the piece nominated by the

gathering... the audience having been previously asked to call out the piece that they would like the dog to pick up.

If no one shouts for the piece you want, you can bluff and say, "Okay then, the Black King it is!" (you can only do this with a relatively large audience) and immediately send your dog out, using your hand to remind the dog of your scent. I have chosen the Black King because there is a strong probability that someone will nominate this one. Studies have shown that there is a considerable likelihood that (strong) black is more often chosen over (wishy-washy) white. Also, the King is more known to non-chess players, and King is an 'important' name as well.

You could always use the 'forced choice' as above instead for other pieces. You may well want to use the Castle because it is on a corner, and easier for the dog to retrieve.

Tracking — the Roy Hunter Way

Most dogs can and do already track. That is: the dog can follow where another dog or animal has walked. Here the dog is being judged not on accuracy but rather on results (from a practical point of view). If a dog did not catch up with his quarry most of the time, he would starve to death and there would be no dogs! Thus, when the dog is following another creature in the wild environment, he may well track some of the time, wind (or air) scent at others, and use a combination of both at other times.

From our point of view, we need the dog to keep religiously on the track following footprint to footprint. (This doesn't have to be a slow process!) Competitions are meant to follow practical exigencies. From a Police point of view, many clues may be lost if the dog wandered about all over the place. The Police need to know the exact route taken by the villain, and if and where he dropped anything along the way.

In Working Trials competition, marks or points are lost for portions of the track missed. In training, if a dog wanders too far from the track, then even the most observant handler may not be able to regain the path. If a dog is allowed (even occasionally) to hunt or trail (as the combination of tracking and air scenting skills is sometimes called), the dog will develop bad habits and never get to become a good tracking dog. **We want to train the dog to stay on the actual track no matter what difficulties or distractions are at hand.** This is achieved by conscientious training.

Let us be clear that on any 'soft' surface (a grass field, a ploughed field, verges, soccer field, recreational ground, etc.) the dog is NOT only tracking the human scent on the ground, but the disturbances to the ground that occur when a person walks over it. Do not believe what you see on television!

When someone walks across a grass field, several things happen. Firstly, the grass is crushed and bruised. Secondly, the soil itself is compressed. And thirdly, microorganisms in the soil are crushed. These three occurrences will differ according to the weight, size of shoe, length of stride, and manner of walking of the individual moving over the ground.

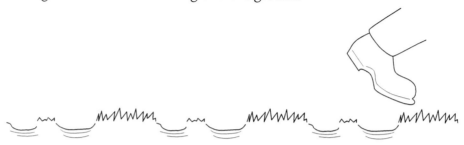

When grass is crushed, it starts to decay. It does not start to decay in six months time—when it is obvious to us—nor in three months or even three minutes. Bacteria start to act on it immediately. This smells different than live, undisturbed grass. Also, when grass is crushed, moisture is released which begins to evaporate, thus making another scent.

Chemical changes take place when soil is crushed (This is so with the crushing of any substance.) When a chemical change takes place a different scent is given off. As with grass, when the surface of the soil is disturbed, moisture is released to evaporate and causes an additional scent. (Apart from weeding, this is the reason that gardeners hoe their plots).

When the organisms in the soil are crushed, two things happen. Body fluids are released and filter to the surface and evaporate while at the same time bacteria start to work on the 'corpses' causing yet another odor.

You can see from this that there are six sources of scent resulting from a person walking across a soft surface which has little to do with that person's own body scent. These six sources will vary in intensity according to the nature of the surface being walked upon. A grass field will give more scent from crushed vegetation than a ploughed field. The ploughed field will be more affected by the crushing and disturbance of the soil itself. Another variable in the amount of scent left is the length of time that different sources reach their peak, and different times for them to disappear (evaporate) altogether.

Because of this variation, a track can be worked by a dog immediately after it has been laid (a person has walked it) or anything up to two days!!! My own Rottweiler once did a track laid by one of my colleagues forty-four and one quarter hours old. A bloodhound enthusiast in Idaho claimed that one of that breed did a track three months old! Believe that if you want...

Weather will affect a track. Strong winds can disperse it or hasten its evaporation. Strong sunshine (especially at midday) deteriorate it rapidly while rain, frost or snow may enhance its length of life.

Equipment for Tracking Training

• initially a six foot leash and a flat buckle collar
• later a nonrestrictive tracking harness and a 30 foot tracking line
• several poles or flags to push into the ground to mark your track (these can be any type of pole easily seen by you—it doesn't matter if the dog can see the poles or not)
• an end-of-track article (something with which you can have a tug-of-war with your dog) such as a short length of nylon rope
• access to one or more fields (however, it is possible to teach a dog to track in a park or even the grass verge of a road)
• a waterproof jacket, leggings and boots
• a supply of treats that your dog really likes (not plain kibble)
• a notebook and pen or pencil to record your progress (make maps)

You will also need enthusiasm and devotion! It is necessary to practice frequently when first training a dog. (I am talking about EVERY DAY for the first two or three weeks.) Practicing daily means that you will need to go out in all kinds of weather.

• a friend who also wants to start a dog tracking is useful, but not essential

• a sense of direction and the ability to walk in a straight line are also important. I'll show you how you can ensure that you do walk in a straight line!

All dogs can track. Some will take longer to respond to training than others. It is important to make sure that you set your dog up for success during each practice session. These early tracks are the building blocks or foundation of your dog's future training.

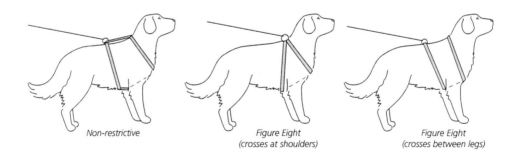

Non-restrictive

Figure Eight
(crosses at shoulders)

Figure Eight
(crosses between legs)

The Figure Eight Tracking Harness

Here are the directions for making the Figure Eight tracking harness with two ways of using it. This harness is similar to the Figure Eight Head

Collar popular here in England. All that is needed to make one is: a length of cotton or nylon webbing about one inch in width, and long enough to go entirely around the dog's neck, cross over the withers, and go around his chest and is held together with a plastic clip (the type used on suitcases and backpacks as well as many dog collars) on his flank.

A metal ring placed at the center of the '8' is used as the fulcrum — where the tracking line is attached. There is also a floating metal ring which can be used as an alternative point for attaching the line. (See Diagram)

After putting the harness on the dog and adjusting it for length, make sure the webbing is flat all the way around. carelessness may result in the webbing being twisted and this will cause discomfort to the dog and a resulting lack of concentration.

This harness is light, soft enough to be carried in your pocket and is also washable. It can be used either way up (see diagram) with the crossover of the '8' being either over his shoulders OR underneath his body. The second alternative has an advantage for dogs just starting to track in the way we want them to... the pressure on the back of the dog's neck from the harness encourages the dog's head towards the ground. The stronger the dog pulls, the more the head is pulled downwards. This is very useful for dogs who want to dash away with their heads in the air. Also, it will slow a dog down.

The Figure Eight tracking harness is not only a training aid (although it can be dispensed with once the dog has developed good tracking habits) it can also be a reserve tracking harness easily carried in trouser pocket. You (or someone competing with you) may one day be pleased that a 'reserve' was available.

Reading Your Dog

We must always be aware of our own dog's reactions when he is (or is not) working. Each dog will give off signals when he is sure of himself (head down, pulling), signals while he is working (a pattern of tail wagging, head set), signals when he is nearing the end of his search (excitement) and signals when he has made a find (body still, tail vibrating). Because dogs vary in their types and amounts of visual signals, it is difficult to assess these signs without a pre-sight into them. A handler at the end of a thirty foot line may only notice the carriage of the tail until other things have been pointed out to him. The tail alone is indeed a great indicator of the dog's mood, sureness or insecurity... but other things will give you clues.

To successfully observe an experienced dog, place other handlers along a track at intervals—far away enough to see clearly, but not close enough to interfere. Place one spectator near the start of observe the dog picking up the track and starting. Place one near an intermediate article, one at a turn, one along the length of a long leg, and one at the end. Each of these handlers is to observe the dog as it passes them—taking note of the tail carriage, the position of the head, the ears, the pressure of the dog against the harness, the dog's eagerness and intensity. (See Diagram.)

Another way to learn to read a dog's behavior is to plan a 'square' track and have all the handlers stand in a group in the middle of the square and observe the dog's progress together. An experienced handler is helpful here to point out all the signals he sees as they happen. (See Diagram.)

The information than can be divulged to the handler who has just finished the track. This is useful to him because it will make him more aware of his dog's reactions AND everyone taking part will become more observant of their own dogs.

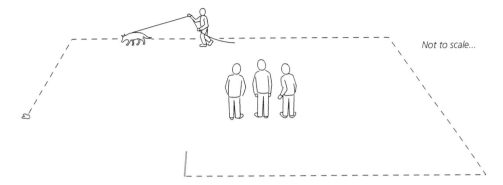

Not to scale...

The Line Drill

Line drill makes handlers more competent at handling the tracking line without messing up the dog in the process!

First, consider how the line is coiled up to be stored in your tracking bag. Many people coil the line around their hand and elbow into a skein (like knitting wool when it is first purchased)—resembling the way rope is coiled in loops. This often gets tangled into "bunches of bananas" when it is thrown out. (See Diagram.)

Skein   *Skein thrown out*

If the line is wound up into a ball (like wool when it is being knitted), then it will never tangle. Start with the loop. Wind it around your fingers a few times and then wind it around itself (tightly). You end up with the clip. (See Diagram next page.)

When you want to track, unwind it a couple of feet, clip the end onto the dog and **throw** the rest away from you. It CANNOT get tangled using this method!

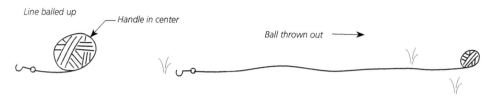

Line balled up

— Handle in center

Ball thrown out ⟶

Now, to practice handling the line! Clip the line to a fence at a level of twelve to fifteen inches off the ground (to simulate the height of a dog). Throw the rest of the line out behind you—holding it well up in the air with one hand and feeding it though with the other hand—work your way backwards to the end of the line. Work forwards to the fence —keeping the line tight all the while, taking up the slack with your other hand.

The line should remain in a straight line between your raised hand and the fence all the time. (See Diagram.) If it varies (slack, tight, slack) then you are not doing it right. Practice going backwards and forwards. A steady pressure is what we are looking for here.

Some dogs need the handler to keep the line high... if the line touches their backs they are finished. Other dogs couldn't care less! If you have a sensitive dog and have a long track to work, your arm will get tired. Now you have to practice changing arms without altering the pressure. While walking toward the fence, simply lift your other arm beside the first and transfer the line over—taking up the slack with the newly relieved arm.

When you are confidently moving back and forth on the fence, you are ready to practice with a person (instead of a dog).

Get a friend who is interested in tracking (or at least interested in dog training)! Clip the line around his or her waist and instruct him/her to walk away from you in the direction you have indicated. Stand still and pay out the line as he or she walks away—keeping a slight pressure between you and your 'dog'. When you have half of the line paid out, start to follow the 'dog'—keeping the pressure on the line. Continue for about twenty yards and stop. Start again and repeat. This exercise is to get you to be able to follow your dog smoothly from the start of the track without jerking him. The wrong way to start a dog is to pay the line all the way out to the end and then start to walk forward. Try the **wrong** way—your assistant will tell you that he feels a slight jerk. Swap positions with your assistant and you become the 'dog'. If your 'real' dog gets a jerk on the line at any time, he may feel he is wrong. With some dogs the feeling is so demoralizing that he will pack up and quit. Other dogs could not care less and will keep pulling. If that's the case, then you are lucky! (See Diagram.)

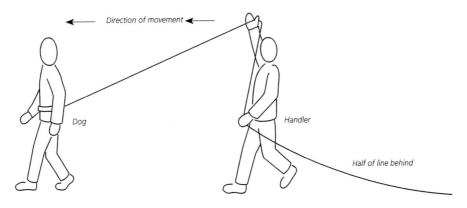

Direction of movement

Dog

Handler

Half of line behind

For the next exercise, try to get your assistant or 'dog' tracking in a straight line and practice veering off to one side of the other. If you give a sudden jerk to get the dog back on the track OR to stop forward progress, you will probably put most dogs off—even the gung-ho type! As your assistant veers off the track about two feet, **gradually** increase your pressure on the line until he can go forward no further. IF you are gentle enough, he will strive to go forward, and in doing so centrifugal force will make him swing to one side or the other. If he continues to veer away from the track, keep the pressure on. But, if he swings back towards the track, ease off the pressure the nearer he gets to the track. When he is on the track he can continue forward as you maintain constant slight pressure while working the track! (See Diagram.)

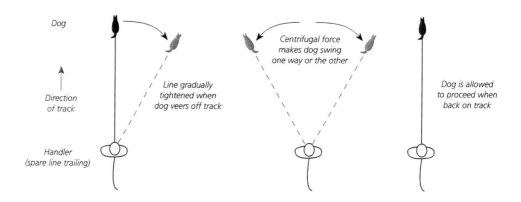

If each of you practice this and swap roles, then you both know what is like to be handler and dog before trying it with (and making mistakes on) a real dog. It is also helpful to practice this 'blind', that is the handler either closes his eyes or wears a blindfold over them. Now the handler cannot see the 'dog', but must rely on the feel of the line alone to tell him what the 'dog' is doing. This exercise quickly points out how important line handling is while still keeping it FUN.

A handler working an experienced dog might blindfold himself on a practice track in order to acquire additional confidence. This technique also helps the handler avoid influencing the dog unduly.

Track Laying Skills

It is obvious—for a person to be able to accurately indicate the track to a dog, **_that person must know exactly where he or she has walked_**. This should not be too difficult while laying the shorter, straight tracks. In reasonably long grass (three to four inches) the track can actually be seen. You can seen it in snow or frost and you can see it on a ploughed field. However, in some circumstances, even the very short tracks cannot be seen.

The reason for the second pole being put in past the end of the track (see Practice Tracks) is to give the track layer something to line up on so that a straight line can be walked. The pole is put in approximately six feet beyond where the article will be placed.

Because you will be laying the majority of the tracks yourself, it is not essential that you have a partner. It is useful however, to have someone with you in the beginning to hold the dog, and later when you and the dog become more experienced to lay the occasional track for you. The reason to have a third party lay tracks infrequently is because **_it is imperative that you know exactly where the track goes in training so that you can put the dog right if he gets hopelessly lost_**. The only person you can truly rely on is yourself, believe me!!! Do yourself a big favor—learn good track laying skills!

When a dog and handler are more experienced, get a trustworthy person to lay the odd track. You MUST learn to rely on and follow the dog and thus become more self-confident in future tracking situations.

Practice Tracks

Track Number One—the 'Ten Yard Track'

Once you get to the field you are using, tease your dog with the article, throw it on the ground, and when he picks it up, have a tug-of-war game. Get the dog to release the article and repeat. It is important to get the dog really excited about the game that comes with the article!

For all of your 'nursery' tracks, you will need to have the wind behind you (coming towards your back) as you lay the track and as you work the dog along the track. Because the air currents down near the ground where the dog is going to track may be moving in a different direction from the air currents higher up, you must determine the wind direction at the lower level. Toss a handful of grass, drop a feather or observe the direction smoke or dust blows near the ground.

Once you have determined the wind direction, either tie your dog to a fence or get a friend to hold the leash so that you are able to walk away from the dog in a straight line with the wind behind you.

Taking two poles and the article with you, walk about six feet away from your dog. Tease the dog with the article. Place one of the poles in the ground and lay a scent pad near the pole. (See Diagram.) This scent pad gives the dog assistance at the start by having intense scent near the pole which diminishes in intensity over three paces until it is the same as the rest of the track.

Stand with your back to the pole (and the wind, if any) and walk out about THREE YARDS taking tiny paces. (See Diagram.) Place each foot just halfway along the preceding foot. Be careful not to scuff your feet because this will disturb the ground differently than the normal pace you will be using when walking the rest of the track.

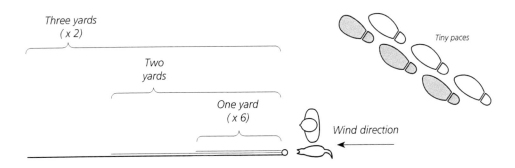

Three yards (x 2)

Two yards

One yard (x 6)

Tiny paces

Wind direction

Now, walk backwards to the pole, and walk out only TWO YARDS taking the tiny steps as before. Back up to the pole again and walk out ONE YARD taking the same tiny steps. (See Diagram.) By now the first yard of the ground nearest the pole has been walked on (compressed) six times, the second yard has been compressed four times, and the third yard just twice. Now you are going to lay your track and this will put two additional layers on top of the first three yards.

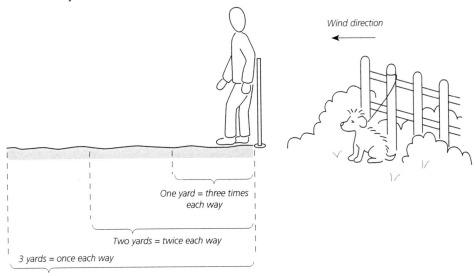

Wind direction

One yard = three times each way

Two yards = twice each way

3 yards = once each way

Tease your dog with the article again and walk out ten yards at a normal pace (your usual stride) allowing your feet to lightly brush the surface of the ground as you proceed.

After ten yards, take another pace leaving your rear leg in position and, reaching out as far as you can—push the other pole into the ground. (See

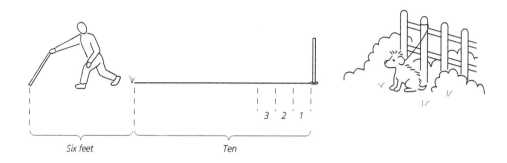

Six feet   Ten

Diagram.) Turn around on the rear leg, face the dog and tease him with the article. Wave the article about, jump up and down, call to him—do anything to make sure you have his interest. (See Diagram.)

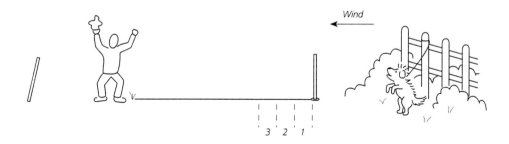

Wind

Place the article flat on the ground in such a way that the dog cannot see it. Put it in a hollow, behind a clump of long grass, or (if there is no way of hiding it) pull up some grass and cover it over. It is important that the dog does not associate the pole with the track or the article. Make sure that you do not place the article at the foot of the pole! (It should be at least six feet away.) Walk back briskly along the track to the dog and bend down at intervals pretending to place something on the ground.

Walking back along the route of the track keeps the dog's attention and is called 'double laying'. Bending over and pretending to place something also helps maintain the dog's interest. (See Diagram.) Quite soon you will be able to eliminate these steps and 'single lay' the track.

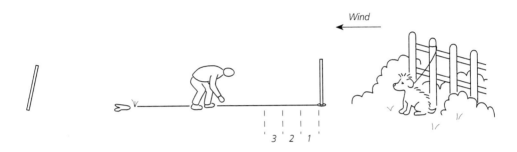

As soon as you get back to the dog, take the leash in your left hand and indicate the track with the back of your right hand in a sweeping movement. Most dogs will smell the ground where you have indicated and start to go forward to investigate the smells on the track that are different from the surrounding ground. If the dog does not go forward, take a pace along the track yourself and indicate the ground to him again. If necessary, you must go all the way along the track in this fashion!!!

Once your dog gets to the end article, EXPLODE with excitement (according to the temperament of your dog) and have a tug-of-war game with him **on that spot**. Some people advocate using a ball or something that can be thrown. I believe that a dog should be rewarded exactly at the end of the track. The tug-of-war simulates the 'kill' he would have made had he been tracking a live quarry.

Using Food in Tracking Training

If your dog shows no interest in the end article, or is interested in the end article only when he finds it (after you have practically guided him to it) but does not put his nose to the ground to get to it, then you need to use food to get your dog interested in the ground and the unusual smell around the treats. Using food does NOT mean putting a tidbit down now and then! Glen R. Johnson (Tracking Dogs—Theory & Method) advocated the systematic process of food use and to be systematic is one of the more important things that I learned from him.

When laying the "ten yard track", place food drops at gradually increasing distances along the track. Make the food drops something the dog really likes and also something that has a distinct scent. Liver and garlic is great (boil or fry the liver with the garlic and leave it soft rather than hard). Another good one is fried, greasy chicken (the kind YOU don't like). Hot dogs, salami and sausages are all good. Cheese is great too, but messy in the summer... Don't make the pieces too large—about the size of your smallest fingernail is ample.

Wipe the ground near the base of the first pole with a morsel. Take one step or pace and bring your other foot up beside the first. Place the first food drop between your feet. (See Diagram.)

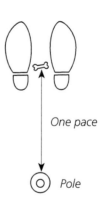

One pace

Pole

Now take two steps, place your feet side by side and place the food treat between them. Repeat after three paces, then take the final four. After taking the extra step to place the second pole and turning around on the back leg, place the article on the ground as before and place three food drops on the article. DO NOT tease the dog as before. It may well be that the dog was over stimulated by the article and that was why the nose did not go down the first time. Time and experience will tell you how much to stimulate the dog, and how long you will need to use food.

As you go back to your dog along the track, bend down at frequent intervals and pretend to put food down on the track. (See Diagram.) This will keep the dog focused (I've been dying to use that word) in the direction and on the ground.

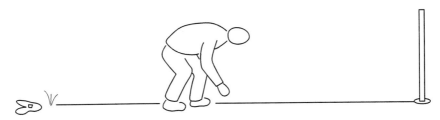

As soon as you get back to the dog, take the leash in the left hand as before and indicate the ground with the back of your right hand in the direction of the track. Make sure he smells the ground near the base of the pole which was wiped with the food morsel. Allow the dog time to consume each morsel. If the dog doesn't proceed forward of his own free will, show him the ground again. He will soon figure it out.

Notice that a total of six portions of food was used for the 'ten yard track'. As a general rule, the same number of food drops will be used even though the tracks get longer—the tidbits will just be spaced further apart. By doing it this way, the dog will have to concentrate on the ground longer for each portion. If the tidbits are evenly spaced the same distance, then the dog would not need to concentrate, but would put the head down every so many paces to eat the food.

To recap, for the 'ten yard track', the food is one yard from the first pole, then three yards, then six yards, then the last three pieces of food are placed on the article at ten yards (the end of the track). (See Diagram.) The dog will eventually realize that there is more food at the end of the track than along it, and may well begin to ignore the ones on the track to get to the feast at the end more quickly.

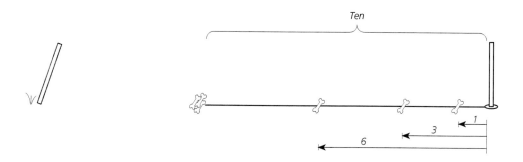

Track Number Two—the 'Twenty Yard Track'

The next track will be laid at twenty yards. Everything is the same—wind direction at your back, first pole stuck in six feet from the dog, scent pad laid (three, two, one yard), the size of the food drops, etc. This time the treats are placed between your feet at two yards from the pole, four yards after that, six after that, and then another eight yards to the end where three pieces of food are placed on the article.

When measuring from the pole, the distance is two yards plus four yards plus six yards, plus eight yards which equals twenty yards. (2 + 4 + 6 + 8 = 20) (See Diagram.)

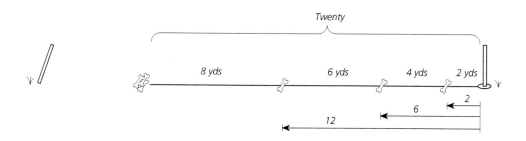

The 'Thirty Yard Track'

The third track you will lay will be thirty yards long. The treats are now placed in three yard units. (See Diagram.) That is: at three yards, then a further six, nine and twelve yards. (3 + 6 + 9 + 12 = 30)

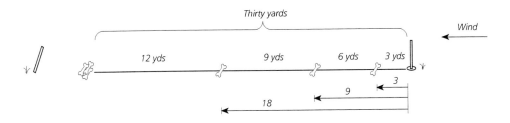

These three tracks will need to be worked on the first day. If the dog does not show much inclination to work them, it may be your fault. You will either need to stimulate the dog more with the article, or (if using food) increase his interest by doing your training an hour after the dog's normal feeding time. Instead of feeding the dog, get the meal ready and offer it to him, then take it away. Offer it twice more in the next hour and take it away twice more. When you go out to lay your track, give him a tasty morsel for 'free' before starting to actually lay the track. This will arouse his interest. When returning along the track, exaggerate your movements when you pretend to put food down... pretend to take food from your mouth, make appreciative noises... you have to be an Actor to train a dog!

Remember: wind behind you. You need the scent of the track or the article to be blown away from the dog. If the wind is coming towards the dog (into his face), the scent will be blown towards him and he will have no need to 'get his head down'. This would develop bad habits.

Remember: the scent pad is the same no matter how long the track. The food drops (if any) are systematically further apart. You run the track with the dog as soon as you return from laying the track. If you stick to these principles and do not try to rush and you will not go wrong.

Some dogs will take to tracking for you straight away and others may appear not to understand what you require. Persevere, do not rush, and I promise YOUR dog will track for you!

The Second Day's Tracks

Once your dog has satisfactorily worked the three "baby" tracks on the first day, then each day you can progress. On the second day you will need to lay a track at twenty yards, one at thirty yards and finally one at forty yards. By now you will feel you are achieving something!

The twenty yard track will be laid and worked in the same way as yesterday's track. The thirty yard track will be different. After you have placed the last pole in the ground, turned on your rear leg and placed the article, jump clear of the track and return to your dog in a half circle instead of going back directly to the dog. (See Diagram.) Work your dog on the track as before... this is called a 'single laid' track.

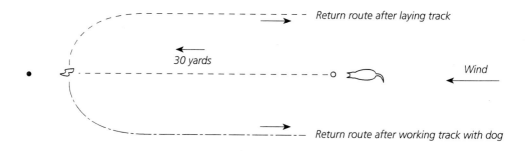

Return route after laying track

30 yards

Wind

Return route after working track with dog

In addition, we now introduce intermediate poles. All it means is that you will place a pole either to the left or right of the track out as far as you can reach. For the twenty yard track, one extra pole will do. As the tracks get longer, more poles can be placed along the track randomly. The reason for the extra poles is that—eventually—you will be using poles to mark a corner or turn in the track. By placing them along the straight track, the dog learns to ignore the poles and will stay on the track. If these intermediate poles were not used early in training, the dog would first be distracted and later learn that a pole meant there was a corner coming up. The intermediate poles also assist the handler stay on the track in the early stages of training.

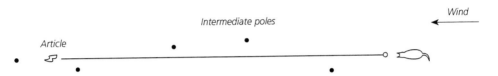

The forty yard track (and all tracks from now on) will be 'single laid' tracks. Lay down the food at four yard intervals on this track. Remember to place a couple of intermediate poles somewhere along the track.

The Rest of the Week

The next day you will again work three tracks: a thirty, a forty, and a fifty yard track. Each following day lay three tracks—starting with the middle length of the day before. Towards the end of the week increase the lengths slightly more. This is the way I advise:

Day One · 10 yards, 20 yards, 30 yards
Day Two · 20 yards, 30 yards, 40 yards
Day Three · 30 yards, 40 yards, 50 yards
Day Four · 40 yards, 50 yards, 65 yards

Day Five	•	50 yards, 65 yards, 80 yards
Day Six	•	65 yards, 80 yards, 100 yards
Day Seven	•	Rest!

If you and your dog have decided by this time that you both like tracking, it is time to purchase a tracking harness. Introduce your dog to the harness gradually at home. Let him wear it while eating... put it on for a few minutes and give him a tidbit... praise the dog and pet him when you put the harness on... play with the dog while he is wearing the harness. Gradually leave it on for longer and longer periods of time. Attach an ordinary leash to it and take the dog for a walk. Once the dog is happy with wearing the harness, it is to be worn only for tracking. Put it on only just before starting the dog working a track. At the end of a track, let the dog eat the food (if still using it) and/or have a tug-of-war. Then, immediately remove the harness. Used in this way, the harness becomes a signal for the dog to track.

Week Two

Start week two by repeating Day Six. The next day do 80 yards, 100 yards and another at 100 yards. On the third day of the second week, just do two tracks at 100 yards and continue in this manner until the end of the week. Take another day off!

Day Eight	•	65 yards, 80 yards, 100 yards
Day Nine	•	80 yards, 100 yards, 100 yards
Day Ten	•	100 yards, 100 yards
Day Eleven	•	100 yards, 100 yards
Day Twelve	•	100 yards, 100 yards
Day Thirteen	•	100 yards, 100 yards
Day Fourteen	•	Rest!

Half way through the second week (say Day Twelve), start approaching the first pole from different angles. (See Diagram.) If a handler always approaches the start exactly in the same direction as the track, the dog will become accustomed to doing just that, and many dogs will rush off down the track without pausing to take the scent. Rushing off wildly down the track is an undesirable trait! If the track doesn't go in that direction, the dog may get confused and not want to try the next time you start him. Instead, allow the dog to work out which way the track goes by himself. To prevent a dog from remembering the direction you walked in, turn him through a circle before taking him to the start pole. Another thing you can

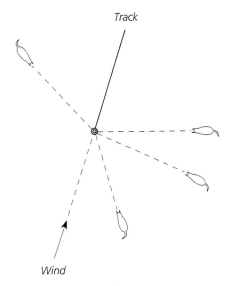

Track

Wind

do early in training is to lay the dog down at the pole to take the scent. (Remember not to always lay him facing the route of the track...)

Week Three and Beyond

If your dog is now enthusiastic—actually pulling you along the track—you are now ready to incorporate turns. Your first turn will be at right angles and to the right. You are also ready for intermediate articles on the track and for tracking through different types of terrain, cross tracks and obstacles. ALWAYS make maps of your tracks! You will then know where you have walked when you return with your dog to run the track. I can't emphasize enough that you know exactly where you have gone so that if your dog does 'go wrong' you are in a position to help him. Also, you must never confuse the dog by THINKING the dog is wrong and acting on that premise when the dog is really right!!!

Turns

When your dog can enthusiastically do a hundred yard track, it is time to introduce turns. Lay a couple of straight (one legged) tracks with the dog out of sight—leaving the dog in the car. These tracks repeat what the dog already knows. NEVER introduce two new things at once—such as turns AND being out of sight. Leave the dog in the car for the majority of the tracks you now do. (If you need to re-motivate your dog, occasionally secure him to the pole so he can see you 'go away'.)

The third track will have a turn at right angles to the first leg and to the right. (See Diagram.) After this you must do left and right turns on a random basis. Most dogs are right-handed—that is, they turn in a clockwise direction when you call them or when 'making their bed'. This is why the first turn is to the right to make it easier for the dog. (If you know your dog is left-handed, then make your first turn to the left.)

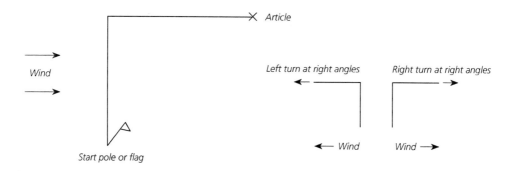

A dog takes scent while inhaling; a dog does not take scent while exhaling. The dog MUST exhale or else he would fall over! Therefore, the dog is not taking in the scent of the track all the time. While the dog is exhaling, he continues along the same line he was walking. If he happens to be exhaling when he passes over a corner, he may ignore it. As soon as he discovers that he is no longer on the track (the next intake of breath), he will cast (go around in a circle) until he cuts into the second leg when inhaling... and then he will continue tracking in the new direction.

You will need to have the wind behind you for the straight tracks (only one leg) and you will need the wind behind you on the second leg (last leg) of the track with a turn. This is important because it will help prevent the dog from lifting his head—which he would do if the scent of the end article was blown towards him. The dog may well 'overshoot' this turn if he was exhaling at the time and tracking fast. (He could

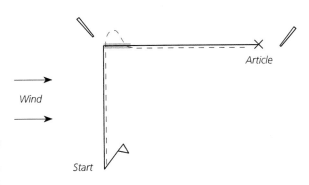

overshoot it to such a length that regaining the track is difficult.) If the wind was behind him on the second leg, the dog would have been tracking downwind on that side so that he would cut into the triple laid part of the second leg and make the turn. (See Diagram.)

Here's how it's done. Lay a track of approximately 50 yards. Line up on two items to your right. Place a pole out to your left as far as you can reach without leaving the track. (See Diagram.) Turn 90° to your right to face the

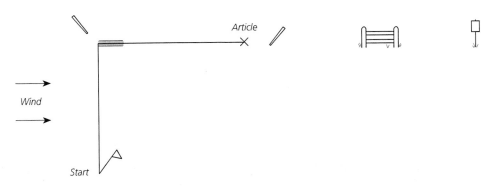

new landmarks. Without hesitating, walk out eight paces... back up to the turn (not the pole) and walk forward again towards the landmarks chosen—another 50 yards.

By backing up to the turn, we have 'triple laid' (walked over three times) the direction of the new leg. This is done in the beginning when first introducing turns to make it easier for the dog. In time, backing up to a corner will be eliminated altogether by phasing it out gradually as follows: triple lay a corner walking normally—single lay a corner by walking heel to toe for the first few yards—gradually increase the length of your stride for the first few paces after a turn—and finally walk normally after a turn.

If you need to stop on the track for any reason (to draw on your map), make sure it is at least 20 paces from the corner or from an article. If you stop at the corner, the increased pressure on the ground at that spot will become a confusing clue to the dog and you will create a large scent pool as well. This makes learning corners unnecessarily difficult for the dog because he will come to rely on this heavier scent.

At the end of the second 50 yards, place the end article and jump clear of the track AND return in a roundabout route. (See Diagram.)

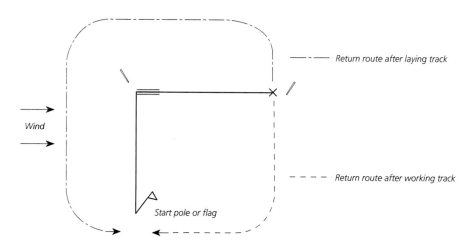

Each new track you lay, increase one leg or the other by ten yards (not both). If your dog is taking to the new task enthusiastically, then these increases may be longer, however—do not run before you can walk! You will be sorry later if you mess your dog up by not giving strong foundation work in the beginning.

By the time you have two legs of 100 yards each, you can introduce a second corner (third leg). Each of these legs will now be reduced to 50 yards and laid in the form of stairs. (See Diagram.) The wind will now be behind you on both the first and last legs.

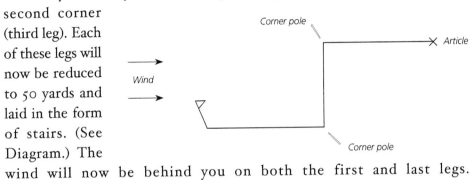

Continue as before. You can make your progress quicker by daily increasing the length of all three legs each time you lay the track. Use your poles to mark the turns and use landmarks to make sure that you walk as straight as possible and help you know exactly where you have walked. Build up the length to three 100 yards legs.

By the time you have gotten to this point (and as long as your dog is still enthusiastic) you are ready to add more turns to each track. It is also time to introduce turns that are less than 90° (more open) and more than 90° (more acute). (See Diagram.)

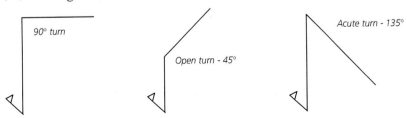

I repeat, ALWAYS carry your map with you and jot down where you have walked. It is essential to know EXACTLY where you have gone so that you can help your dog if he goes wrong. You must never confuse your dog by THINKING he is wrong—and acting on that premise when he is RIGHT.

Continue to place random 'intermediate' poles along these new legs. There may be so many poles now that you may become confused yourself even if you have drawn your map. If this is the case, then put colored tape on the tops of the poles that you are going to use to mark the corners. Alternatively, put the intermediate poles in the ground upright and the corner poles in at an angle—inclined in the new direction.

Intermediate Articles and Article Indication

No matter if we are tracking for fun, in practical situations or for competition, we need to have the dog indicate to us any articles bearing human scent that the dog finds along the track. The articles may be clues (from a Police point of view), valuables belonging to a grateful owner, points gained in a competition, or collectible items in a game.

Whatever the article, it is desirable to teach your dog to indicate to you when he has found such items. When your dog is proficient at tracking for you, you are ready to teach your dog 'intermediate articles' (articles found along a track leading up to the end article).

If you have made enough of a fuss when the dog has recovered the end article of a track, it will be relatively easy. There are various methods used by different handlers. Some continue to use large articles and end the track at each— starting a 'new' track where the last article was. Others gradually reduce the size of the end article so that the dog gets used to indicating smaller items. And, others mark the place where each intermediate article is and force the dog to stop over it with pressure on the line before going to town with praise.

Personally, I go out and lay a track with many small articles along it. I then work the track with the dog. When the dog goes over the top of any (ignoring them), I say nothing. Sooner or later he will discover one or some. As the dog stands still and sniffs the ground, I say "Stand. What have you got? Stand." gently and encouragingly. I move up to him quickly (not too fast initially because I don't want to alarm 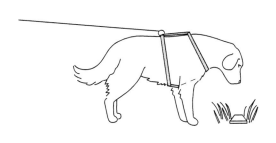 him) while encouraging him to remain standing all the time. Then, I really praise him. If the dog has picked the article up, I gently take it before praising. (I really don't want my dog to pick up any articles. I'll explain why later.)

During the course of a 200 yard track, the dog may have found four out of the ten articles I put down. I go out afterwards and pick up the other six. (This is good training for track laying!) At this stage it does not matter that the dog has missed some of the articles. The point is that the dog got a reward for each of the ones he found! Soon the dog will be alert for items on the track and the resulting approval from the handler. The dog will become conscious of what is required without the slightest hint of negative training.

In England, the Judge in competitions will ask you how your dog indicates articles. Some handlers have been rebuffed by the Judge for replying, "Well, my dog may sit, or he might stand over the item, or he may lie down on the article, or he might pick it up, or sometimes he just dips his head and hesitates slightly." The Judge wants to know exactly what your dog does, and so do you!

A dog should be taught one particular way of indicating articles. Picking the item up is easy to train if your dog likes to retrieve. However, the dog may pick up the article and continue along the track... neither you or the Judge may have noticed... and the dog may drop it later without you realizing. There have been cases of dogs swallowing articles along the track. If your dog is not trained to sit after picking up an article, the dog may wander off the track completely.

Sitting or laying down on the articles seems okay, but sometimes the ground is a finely ploughed field (for example) and the article is pushed into the soil. If a dog is taught to lie down, it is best if he lays down just before the article without touching it at all.

For myself, standing over the article is the best way. It is not the easiest to train because it is easy for the dog to move forward when standing than from the other positions. However, you can see from my teachings that the dog has been taught to stand over the articles right from the beginning. If the reward is strong enough, the dog will develop a strong habit.

The articles that you choose to place on your FUN tracks are up to you—*it is **the amount of scent on the articles that matters, not the size !***

In English Trials, the regulations for both the track and search articles states that they should be about the size of a matchbox or a six inch nail, and that they should not be injurious to the dog (such as glass or sharp metal) or small enough to encourage swallowing. One eccentric (I say stupid) Judge was renowned for using articles so small that all seven— three from a TD track and four in the Search Square—would all fit into a match box! Eventually, after some dogs were injured by swallowing small caliber cartridge cases and the flip tops of lemonade bottles, the Kennel Club insisted on seeing all articles used.

I have used some of the following articles: lengths of leather cut from an old leash, knotted lengths of rope or cord, pieces of denim or toweling, old dessert spoons, beer mats or coasters, pine cones, pieces of identifiable wood, clothes pins (both plastic and wooden), wadded up paper, metal or plastic jar tops, small tin cans, cassette tape cases, a toy truck or car, a pair of cheap sunglasses... use your imagination!

Tracking on Different Terrain

The amount and type of vegetation can make a dog's task easier or harder. With sparse vegetation on hard ground, the dog must concentrate very hard. In contrast, lush, four inch high, damp, green grass makes the job easy for most dogs.

In England, Suburban Police Dogs have to track on various hard surfaces—roads in towns, runways on airfields, etc. It has always been thought that dogs can only do this type of tracking on a relatively fresh track under good conditions (no wind and little other traffic about). In Police Dog competitions, the "Hard Surface Track" is only a half hour old. Practical tracks have been worked at a much older time by some dogs in London, and now in the United States there is a new competition: Variable Surface Tracking in which different sorts of surfaces can be found on one track, which can include black top or tarmac, dirt, concrete, sand as well as different types of vegetation—depending on where the test is given.

A ploughed field (providing it has been standing a few days) is relatively easy for dogs even though there is no vegetation. A freshly ploughed field (or newly mown grass) is extremely difficult. As a person walks from one surface to another, the vegetation, soil, etc. (and the scent thereof) that sticks to the shoes will be deposited on the new surface for a certain distance (varying according to conditions). This gradually peters out, but gives the dog enough time to acclimatize himself to the elements of the new surface. The human factor (length and heaviness of stride) is there all the time. The influence of the of the individual scent of the track layer is minimal (other than on hard surfaces). (See Diagram.)

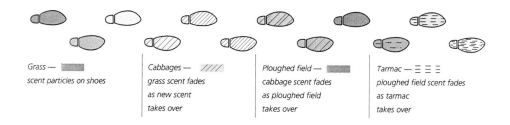

Grass — ▓▓▓	Cabbages — /////	Ploughed field — ▓▓▓	Tarmac — ☰ ☰ ☰
scent particles on shoes	grass scent fades as new scent takes over	cabbage scent fades as ploughed field takes over	ploughed field scent fades as tarmac takes over

The type of surface and the attitude of the dog will also determine the length of line that you pay out. On a hard surface or a short grass field, you can allow the whole of your line (normally around 30 feet) to be paid out. If there are a lot of heavy clumps of long grass or bushes scattered about, the line needs to be held shorter and kept high. In the woods with the trees close up, the line will have to be very short. Any entanglement on natural obstacles may result in jerking the dog—and some dogs are so sensitive that a jerk may put them off. Other dogs could not care less and have the attitude of "Let's get on with the track!"

Hedges or walls alongside a field can affect the track if they vary at all (have gaps, are of different heights). A wind blowing from a hedge to the track will 'move the track over' opposite a gap. (See Diagram.)

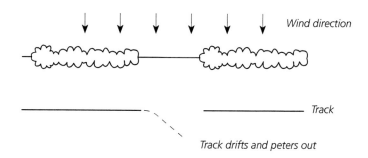

Wind direction

Track

Track drifts and peters out

If there is only an occasional part of a hedge or wall and the wind blows from it to the track, the bulk of the track will be 'moved over'... and where the all obstructs the wind, the track will be accurate.

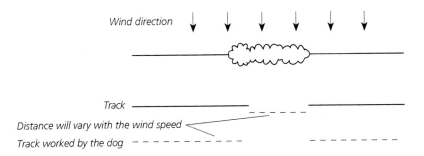

Wind direction

Track

Distance will vary with the wind speed

Track worked by the dog

The slope of the land may affect a track. In very hot weather, as the hot air rises, so will the elements of the track that the dog is using. On a steep slope the dog may well be tracking four or five feet above the ground where the track layer walked. In cooler weather the opposite may happen—the dog may work a track slightly below the track layers path.

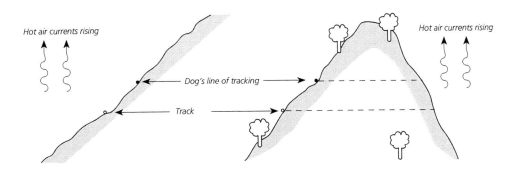

Hot air currents rising

Dog's line of tracking

Track

Hot air currents rising

When working a track with your dog, be aware of all surrounding conditions, the weather and all the things around you. In practice, it is a good idea to teach yourself to look at a clump of grass, a weed, or a stone in the distance and try to estimate how far it is away. With practice, you can become quite accurate and become very aware of your surroundings.

Weather does affect tracks, but not necessarily adversely! Damp still weather will help a dog track. The enemies of a track are very strong winds AND very hot sunshine. Rain is not an enemy—it helps keep the track viable. Very dry weather does not help, but damp, sultry weather does because this brings in the humidity factor.

Do not be put off attempting any track because of conditions. Each dog is and individual, each track is an individual, and both can vary at any specific time. If you track your dog only on still days, he will not know how to track on windy days. By giving your dog as much variety as possible, you are building up his experience level. Good experiences build confidence.

Obstacles on the Track

On a track, the track layer (helper or criminal!) may well negotiate various obstacles either because they are in the way, or in an attempt to foil pursuit by a tracker dog. The obstacles could be in the form of a fence, a stream, a ditch, or even a building.

I used to enlist the help of my neighbor (a young boy) who would lay me a track in our local park on his way to school—leaving a sock at the end. One day, the track stopped at a tree which had a rope ladder going up it and a rope walkway to another tree about thirty yards away. It was 'proved' fifty years ago that a dog cannot track a person suspended more than two feet from the ground (except a bicycle, which is in continuous contact with the ground and impacting the environment the same as a footprint). Anyway I took my dog Tammy (after Tammy Wynette) to the other tree and tracked on from there, recovering the sock.

If your dog comes up to a fence across the track, make him wait until you go up to him, unclip the tracking line (it could get caught), climb over the fence yourself, and call him to you if the fence is easy enough to negotiate. If

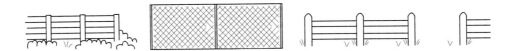

the dog needs your assistance, help him over the fence and put him in a down on the other side until you rejoin him and reattach the line and continue tracking. If the fence is not negotiable by either of you, mark the position so that it can be seen from the other side, remove the harness and line and search for an alternate way around. If you can get through, over or under any place else, do so and return on the other side to the place you have marked. Put the harness and line back on and continue tracking.

To train for such eventualities as the above (and the following ones), get the trained dog used to having a track interrupted. You can achieve this by giving the dog a break along the track. When I visited the Dutch Police Dog Nosework School in 1971, I was shown many demonstrations. One elderly Police Dog Handler (he must have been 95 or thereabouts then) did a track for me with his Shepherd. At that time the Dutch Police did not use a harness or long line—using a fifteen foot rope leash which doubled as a tracking line by taking it out behind the right front leg. After following about 200 yards of a track, the Dutchman put his dog in a down on the track, went to a nearby rock, sat down, loaded his pipe and smoked for five minutes. He then got up, returned to the dog and continued tracking successfully. You could start off by doing this, although you don't have to smoke! Then you can extend the interruption—marking the track where you left it and taking the dog with you. Remove the harness and line and replace it when you take the dog back to the track. You can practice all sorts of interruptions before introducing obstacles.

If the track layer enters a stream to try to put the dog off, do not worry. If the stream is slow-flowing, the disturbances caused by a person walking therein will remain on the surface for some time. The dog will pick up on the disturbances and the human scent lurking in the air. If the stream is narrow, the vegetation on the sides will be disturbed by the person brushing against it. If the stream is fast-flowing and wide enough so that the vegetation is undisturbed, then you must investigate in order to find where the person came out. Search the far bank in both directions until either your dog scents or you see where the track layer has emerged. Bear in mind that a person can come out on the same side as they enter!

If the person you are tracking jumped across a ditch, take up some slack on the line so that when the dog jumps the ditch, he is not pulled backwards. If the track does not continue on the other side, then the person as jumped into and not over the ditch. Put your dog into the bottom of the ditch and allow him to investigate both ways.

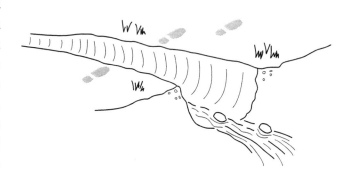

In the event that a building has been entered, you dog may well continue to track. The scent of the environment on the person's shoes diminishes slowly. By the time it has all gone, the dog will have associated it with the body scent of the track layer and continue tracking/searching using this information. If the conditions are such that your dog cannot do this, take the dog outside and walk him around the building so he can (hopefully) pick up the track where the person has come out. If there is no track coming away, then the person is still in the building. Take the line and harness off the dog and encourage the dog to do a building search (as described in the section on searches).

Track Laying Do's and Don'ts

There are definite skills to laying a track; there are both desirable and undesirable methods. Here is a list of things to do and things to avoid:

• DO: walk in a straight line. Get in the habit right from the beginning of lining up on two stationary items (fence posts, telephone poles, gates, corners of buildings...)

• DO: know EXACTLY where you have laid your track... every single footprint!

• DO: walk naturally (apart from brushing your feet over the surface of the ground for the dog's initial tracks) at your normal pace.

• DO: lay each track in one field or area with the same cover initially. If the surface of the field or area varies (grass, ploughed, gravel, macadam), walk on only one surface for any one track until the dog is experienced with each surface separately.

• DO: have the wind behind you on a single leg track AND when you have corners, on the last leg of the track.

• DO: approach the start pole or flag from a different angle to the direction in which you intend laying a track. (See Diagram.)

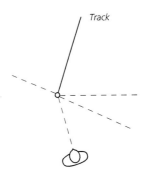

Track

• DO: try to judge the number of paces that you are from any component on the ground. Count off your paces as you walk. This habit will make you more conscious of where you are walking and of distances.

• DO: praise and reward the dog for finishing the track and indicating the article. Remove the harness immediately after praising to signal to the dog that he is finished working.

• If the wind changes (after you have laid your beginner tracks), abort the track and lay a new one in the new direction so that the wind is at your back. Side winds are as dangerous in training (in the beginning) as head winds to the inexperienced dog.

• DO NOT: scrape or scuff your feet along the ground.

• DO NOT: worry if someone (or another dog or animal) has previously walked where you want to lay your track, even if it was only a few minutes before.

• DO NOT: worry if someone walks across your track after you have laid it. Your dog will learn to ignore all these "cross tracks".

• DO NOT: use anything that can move such as a car, cow or airplane! (See Diagram.) Get one item slightly behind the other with an edge showing. Keep these items in the same perspective to each other as you walk forward.

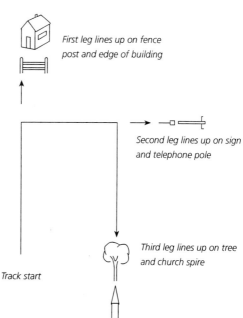

First leg lines up on fence post and edge of building

Second leg lines up on sign and telephone pole

Third leg lines up on tree and church spire

Track start

• DO NOT: use details on the ground to line up on unless they are one-of-a-kind items such as the only rock in the field. I guarantee that if you line up on a clump of daisies that another twenty clumps will have popped up in the meantime by the time you run the track with your dog! However, you can use these indicators in conjunction with your lineup items.

• DO NOT: lay your tracks close to and parallel with the edge of a field. (See Diagram.)

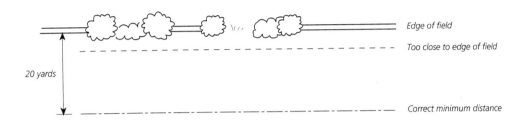

• DO NOT: lay your tracks so that they end at the end of a hedge or end of a field. (See Diagram.)

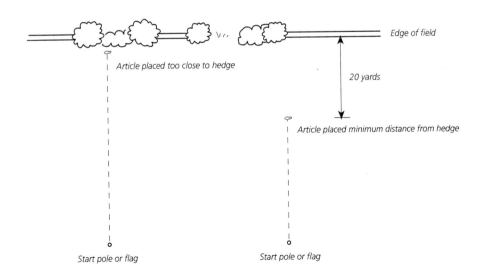

• DO NOT: end a track at a solitary item (such as a lone tree) in a field. (See Diagram.) It is important that the dog not associate the end of the track with something he can see easily or he will learn to rush out to the nearest tree to see if the article is there rather than using his nose to find it.

Article

Incorrect to end a track
at a solitary object

Start pole or flag

Incorrect to use a solitary object
as a turning point

Start pole or flag

• DO NOT: allow the dog to track on after finding the end article.

Cross Tracks

Many handlers are put off by cross tracks. Note that I say handlers. The dog may not be bothered at all unless the handler is uneasy. If there are cross tracks on a track and the handler is unaware of this, he does not upset his dog who would normally cope well.

I have done many experiments with cross tracks. Dogs do vary. Many are track-sure (remaining loyal to the track they started on). Others are track-happy and will follow contentedly (nay EAGERLY) along any track that appears. Luckily, these track-happy dogs can be trained to become track-sure.

Cross tracks can be from humans or animals. Cross tracks can be older than OR fresher than the track we set for the dog. Apart from the time element, cross tracks can be stronger than or weaker than the original. Cross tracks can be more interesting to the dog than the one he is on!

If a dog is exhaling as he passes a cross track, he may be unaware of it. A dog may be aware of a cross track, but be so track-sure that he remains true to the original even though he knows the track is there. (He may make no visible indication of the cross track even though he is aware of it.) Alternatively, he may indicate the cross track to a greater or lesser degree—maybe by just turning his head as he passes it. The dog may investigate it by going along it for a few feet before discarding it and returning to the original. However, there are some dogs who decide, "This one's for me! Whoopee, let's go!"

Fun with Cross Tracks

I have learned fun ways to teach a dog to ignore cross tracks. It is interesting to try all the deliberate cross tracks after a dog has been so trained.

Try this! Lay a track with four parallel legs each 150 yards long and joined by three legs of about thirty yards. (See Diagram.) Use poles to mark

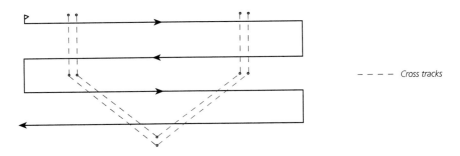

$- - - -$ Cross tracks

where you want the cross tracks to be laid (away from the sides of the original track).

Now get TWO people to walk across it in the manner shown in the diagram. They should try to remain about ten feet apart all the while. I use two people because if a dog is exhaling as he crosses one of these secondary tracks, he will be unaware of it. With two people it is unlikely that he will be exhaling over both of the cross tracks, so we can make sure that the dog is aware of the presence of one or the other.

The cross track layers need not be experienced. However, they should be clearly briefed as to where and how to follow the route you have already marked with poles away from the sides of the original track. No intermediate poles are used to decrease confusion to the cross track layers.

Cross tracks can be made easier or harder to negotiate according to the following factors:

1. The **time** the cross track is laid compared to the original. The closer the time to the original, the more difficult it is to discriminate between them. Cross tracks laid before the 'true track' are less confusing, and the longer before, the less confusing. Cross tracks laid after the original may be more tempting to a dog because some dogs have learned to prefer a fresh track.

2. the **angle** that the cross track passes over the original is important. 90° angles are the easiest and narrow or acute angles are more difficult. (See Diagram.)

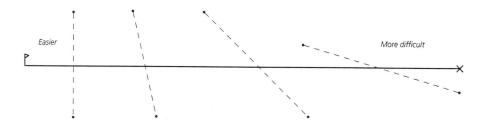

3. The **physical likenesses** of the parties laying both the original or cross tracks are important. (See: Laying your own cross tracks.) If the second track layer is the same weight, has the same leg length (stride), and the same size shoe as the first, then this will make it harder for the dog to distinguish than if one or more of these qualities were different. Although every person lays a different track, some are more different than others!

4. If all the **physical elements** of the track (ground, foliage, weather, humidity) make the actual track hard going, then the dog will more likely ignore the presence of cross tracks because he has to concentrate more on the original track.

In training, the tracks should be laid so that the dog has at least thirty yards on the true track before the second (cross) tracks passes over it. We want the dog to "get the original track in his nose" and thus in his brain before encountering interference.

Laying Your Own Cross Tracks

I read in a doggy magazine once about a lady who laid her own track for her dog, and then loaded herself up with two heavy suitcases in order to lay her own cross tracks. Wow! She did indeed make things easier for her dog, but she was punishing herself unnecessarily. In any case "harder is easier".

Train your dog under the hardest available conditions—where you have the chance to put your dog right should he go wrong. Later, when you yourself are unaware of other cross tracks or obstacles, the dog will have an easier time because he has already experienced more difficult ones in training.

Try these first track patterns to prove it to yourself. (See Diagram.)

With these patterns, you can make sure that the dog is actually tracking (taking scent) as he goes over the cross track(s) by doubling or tripling the cross tracks about ten feet apart at any or all of the crosses. (See Diagram.)

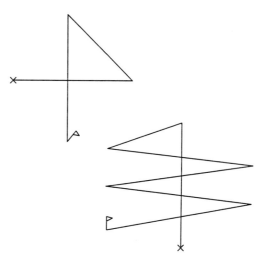

Another interesting experiment you can do is to lay a straight track, and bring your dog into the middle to find the track. (See Diagram.) You will notice that the vast majority of dogs (we can never say ALL in anything to do with dogs) will track in the correct direction straight away OR go the wrong direction (back track) for a few yards and then turn and go the right way.

You can also try doing this by laying a circular track and cutting the ring somewhere along the circumference. (See Diagram.)

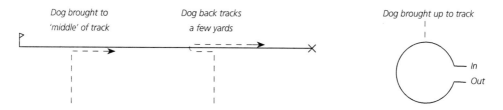

Dog brought to 'middle' of track

Dog back tracks a few yards

Dog brought up to track

In
Out

Having said that if a track is laid from A to B and we start the dog at B, he will track back to A (back track). When I was a Police Dog Handler in London, I was called to a burglary. My Rottweiler picked up a track from the rear fence of the property and tracked to another house 100 yards away. I noticed there was someone in the house and I was very pleased that I had caught up with the burglar. The person was, in fact, the homeowner who had just returned home and had just that minute phoned the police. He thought we were very efficient to get there so soon!!! By talking to each victim, I found that the dog had tracked from the second to the first burglary. After that I experimented laying practice tracks and found that dogs will back track if started at the end, but track in the 'right' direction if started in the middle. (See Diagram.)

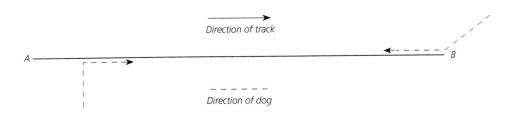

Train for Difficulties, or, Harder is Easier

If a dog never goes wrong in training, he may become confused if in a competition or on an operational track. We should try to make sure that the dog never goes wrong in initial training, BUT once the dog is completely competent and enthusiastic, then it is a good policy to deliberately make him go wrong under controlled circumstances where we can put him right. Lay your own tracks to do this! Line up on two items and lay a straight track with the wind behind you. After 100 yards, put in a pole and walk straight ahead for a further 8 yards (or the full length of your tracking line). Stop and back up to the pole. Turn left 160°, remove the pole and lay another straight leg for 100 yards. Place your end article and jump clear of the track to the right. Return by a roundabout route. (See Diagram.)

When you come up to the track with your dog, you will find that the dog will track the first leg to the very end and will probably (if the wind is still behind you) go on another two, three or four yards—past where you started to walk backwards. He will then probably start to cast to his right.

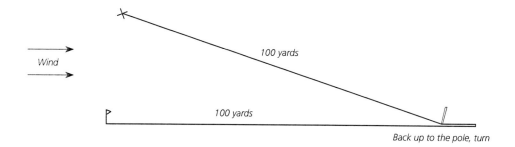

100 yards

Wind

100 yards

Back up to the pole, turn

If you know that he has gone on too far (and cannot possibly cut back to the second leg because he doesn't have enough line to enable him to do so) then you must back up towards the turn. This is good training for the handler for when the dog has lost the track and you don't know where it goes.

As the dog starts to cast, turn 90° to your right. You will now be able to see over your shoulder when the dog cuts into the second leg. If the dog goes straight over it, turn again another 90° so that you are facing back the way you came. Watch the dog. If he cuts the second leg (or if he shows ANY sign of recognizing it) encourage him. ***Important: the first time you try this experiment must be the ONLY time the gets praise or encouragement.*** If you keep praising the dog every time he works out a problem, then you will be creating a situation where he waits for your approval before continuing. Keep your pressure on the line and when he says "Let's go!", then you go with him.

Now, the reason I have told you to turn to your right is that if you always face in the correct direction of the track when you know the way the track goes, the dog will quickly pick up on this and be influenced by your body language. When you come to the situation of running blind (unknown) tracks, then your dog may think that you know best and will try to go in the direction you are facing. In this case, the dog's willingness to please the handler overrides his confidence in himself and his ability to make independent decisions.

Hard Surface Tracking

When I was at the Metropolitan Police Dog Section we used to train dogs and handlers on 'hard surfaces', after all that is what 95% of the ground in London is made up of! As well as for practical use, Hard Surface Tracking was one of the exercises in Police Dog Trials both locally and nationally.

I have been reliably informed that the Hard Surface Track is no longer a required exercise in the Trials these days. It had been reduced from thirty minutes to twenty because ideal conditions were required for it, and it depended to much on the 'luck of the draw' as to whether one got good conditions or bad. Luck plays a part in all competitions, but on the Hard Surface Track it meant a complete failure... and since you had to obtain 70% of the marks available in each section of the competition, then you could not qualify, let alone win! The test has been done away with entirely because locations for the competitions were becoming increasingly hard to find. The HST was both trained and competed on World War Two Aerodromes which were built for the huge bomber planes — some had runways nearly a quarter-mile wide. Most of these have disappeared and now have housing estates built on them. Others are now in use for civilian airlines.

Of course, dogs are still taught to track on hard surfaces. The requirement is 30 minutes at the end of the training course. The course is fourteen weeks long, but all the other things a police dog needs to know are being taught at the same time.

For a dog to track on the streets of a large city, ideal conditions are required. Obviously a dog cannot track then there are great crowds of people walking all over a track he is asked to follow. Heavy vehicular traffic will pollute the air. Windy conditions will adversely affect his chances. If the sun was hot during the day and it is a cool night before, the scent will soon disperse as the ground will be hotter than the air above it.

Favorable conditions are:
- no or few pedestrians both when the track was laid and when the dog is trying to follow the scent
- light vehicular traffic
- a fine drizzle (even a heavy rain is preferable to bone dry conditions)
- a windless night
- that the villain (track layer) has well-worn footwear
- that the ground conditions are colder than the air above it
- the sooner the dog is brought to the scene, the better
- the footway surface is rough rather than smooth (thus holding more scent AND wearing miniscule portions of the footwear away)
- that there is SOME vegetation present (e.g. growing in the cracks of the hard surface
- the villain (track layer) has a distinctive odor

I do not mean that the person belongs to the 'great unwashed', but that his job or surrounding leave him with a definite scent. For example, a gas station attendant, a fish salesman, etc. Certain eating habits also give a person a certain odor e.g. strong curries or garlic.

Although HST was taught up to one half hour, if all the good conditions above were present, tracks much older have been successfully carried out by competent dogs with persistent handlers.

Training Hard Surface Tracking

In the 1950's and 60's, the City of Nottingham was successful in teaching hard surface tracking by teaching hard surfaces BEFORE going on to the much easier soft surfaces. This is still a most successful technique today.

Essentially, train the hard surface the same way you would for other types of tracking, but DO IT FIRST. Begin with short tracks. You can spray or squirt water along the track as you go and walk through it if you want. Water will help hold some additional scent. Make your steps shorter than normal, and at first drag your feet along the track as well in order to deposit some of the material from the bottom of your footwear. Some types of hard surface hold scent better than others such as brick and grainy concrete.

Once your dog has reached a satisfactory proficiency on a hard surface, then you can add open corners and simple obstacles such as a curb. Gradually increase the length of the track, the time, and the difficulty, BUT NOT AT

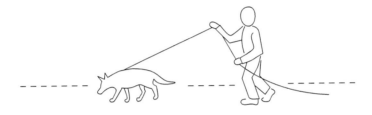

THE SAME TIME. Increase only one requirement at a time else you discourage your dog or encourage bad habits. Be sure to work rather closely behind your dog during this learning process... no more than six to eight feet (depending on the size of the dog). By keeping closer to your dog than allowed in competitions, you are in a position to notice quickly if the dog is going too far off the track. Restrain the dog gently.

There is a world of difference in the requirements of any form of tracking in a competition, and the needs of actual "Operational Tracking". In competition, there must be certain standards demanded in order for the Judge to balance one performance against another. In operational tracking, the end result is all that matters... did the dog lead the handler to the burglar? ...did the dog recover and property or evidence enroute? Here it doesn't matter if the dog followed actual footprints, followed the air-scent above the footprints, or if he followed air scent blown against a wall, hedge, building or curb. It matters not if the dog and handler, working together and using past experience, cut out a degree of the track to pick it up further on... what matters is the end result.

By the time your dog is working a half hour old track that is 3-400 yards in length, you can begin working soft surfaces by starting the process all over again. Remember: each surface must be taught separately to the dog. The larger the variety of surfaces the dog has experiences on, the better the dog will be.

Distraction Training

If you deliberately train with distractions, your dog will be able to concentrate more when you come upon distractions accidentally along the track. Distractions can come in the form of other people walking near, parallel or across the track while your dog is actually tracking. The same can happen with other animals—with or without human accompaniment.

Distractions can be in the form of garbage all around the track. For some dogs it could be feces—try tracking through a cattle field for a dog who likes to eat meadow muffins! One or two muffins are tempting, but a field full is too much.

Birds disturb many dogs—either triggering a hunting instinct or a defensive move. Consistently working through distractions make the distractions less powerful and less overwhelming to the dog. The same distractions can come in the form of feathers or paper blowing about.

If you train with these things (set them up on purpose), then not only will your dog NOT be taken by surprise the first time they happen, he will also concentrate more on the track once you have made it worth his while. Make the end of the track so exciting that the distractions fade into insignificance.

You can have a lot of fun with tracking... give your dog and yourself a new challenge!

In Closing

Having fun with your dog's wonderful sense of smell has several bonuses. Your dog will enjoy working with you and you will appreciate your dog more when he can do something that you could never learn to do—no matter how hard you try!

You can continue to train your dog to do things that you require without the boredom (for dog and handler) of strict obedience routines. Remember, each time your dog does as you tell him, you are enhancing your authority—even though the dog enjoys what he is doing! What a lovely way to overcome a dominant dog!

As well as training, we can open up our horizons in competitions. In England we need to find articles, people, to track in Working Trials, and to do scent in our obedience. In the USA (at the moment) only tracking and scent are required in competition. All of these things can be of practical use AND can also have entertainment value. No matter how you use them, keep things lighthearted. Frequently go back to your FUN methods and always keep a FUN outlook.

I began this book with a reference to my Nosework Courses and being asked to write a book by the people who have attended. I so enjoy training this particular course—probably my favorite—and would like to say now that I have enjoyed writing about Nosework as well. It has been FUN to do!

Appendix: Foundation Exercises

Alert by Barking

The foundation for this is simply teaching a dog to speak on command! Whenever your dog barks spontaneously (someone passes your house, a person rings the doorbell, when you fix the dog's food), encourage it. Say in an excited voice, Good Dog, SPEAK! If he continues to bark, praise him and reinforce, Good Dog, SPEAK! If you have told the dog off in the past for barking, just say 'good dog' softly at first—introduce 'speak' only when you are sure he knows you approve.

At first, the dog probably will stop when you first command him, or only give one more bark. Keep at it. Once he is barking at least one time for every command you give, pop him a treat and command again. When he realizes that he can get a treat for barking, you can withhold the treat until he barks twice. Gradually demand longer continued barking for one treat. Work up to ten or even twenty. You can show him that you have a treat in your hand, but don't get into the habit of holding it up because that can eventually become a signal that you may not be able to get rid of!

Practice speaking on command in a variety of other places. If you don't, the dog may think he can only bark in one specific place and it may prove difficult to get him to speak elsewhere. The more methods and places you use, the more the dog will realize that it is the word SPEAK that counts. Have the dog respond to the command SPEAK from another handler as well. This is helpful in practicing searching for people.

If your dog rarely speaks spontaneously, then another approach must be made. Get the dog excited by holding his food up high... tease him by pretending to throw a toy and then not throwing it... tie the dog up and then go out of sight and call him... hide in an inaccessible place and call him... get another dog to bark in his presence. (Also refer to the section on Irretrievable Objects.) If he barks for any of these reasons, keep it going. Some dogs find this an easy exercise and some dogs find it harder.

Play Rewards

Anglo American Dog Training recognizes five rewards that we can give our dog for doing what we want. Because they all begin with the letter P, they are called the Five P's. They are:

- **P**raise, verbal
- **P**et, physical
- **P**op, give a food treat
- **P**lay, a game
- **P**leasant expression on your face!

These are gone into more deeply in my books ***Fun and Games with Dogs,*** and ***MORE Fun and Games with Dogs***, also published by Howln Moon Press. For this exercise, we are concerned with play.

The vast majority of dogs LOVE to play in some form. It is probably THE most important of all the P's for a well-fed dog. (Popping is obviously more important for a hungry dog and is also more desirable to use for slow or stationary exercise than Play, which is too exciting.)

Play can involve many forms: 'dancing' with your dog, just running with the dog, throwing things for the dog to chase and retrieve, or having a tug-of-war. You can make 'heelwork' into a game by trying to lose the dog from your side... Jumping is so exciting to your dog that you can call this a game... Other parts of agility (such as weave poles) may not initially be exciting for the dog, but can be made so by tossing a ball as the dog finishes the exercise...

Some dogs have never learned to play such as those whose mother did not let them or those who were placed at an early age with staid owners. (Notice that I did not say OLD owners! Many older people are also FUN people and many thirty year olds are boring—to a dog!) Even so, most of these dogs can be taught to play. The best time to get a dog to play is when it is naturally more excitable—when you first get up in the morning—when you return home from having been out (it does not matter if it's five minutes or five hours) the dog will be excited at your return. Have a 'chase article' conveniently left near where you and the dog will be reunited and throw it for him straight away. Hopefully the chase instinct will come into play. He may not pick it up right away, but if he shows any interest at all, this can be developed.

Retrieving

Although you don't need the precision required in obedience 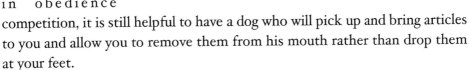 competition, it is still helpful to have a dog who will pick up and bring articles to you and allow you to remove them from his mouth rather than drop them at your feet.

Try using any or all of the following methods to get a happy and reliable retrieve. Do not hurry. Do not get impatient. Do not use negative commands

(NO!), negative attitudes (stupid dog!), or even negative thoughts (I can't get him to do it!). Remember the Five P's outlined in the Basic Training section.

Spontaneous Retrieving

Anytime your dog goes to pick something up, softly command him PICK IT UP! Go to him slowly, stroke his chest, praise him... and try to keep the item in his mouth (your forearm can stop his bottom jaw from opening with practice). After a few seconds, say THANK YOU and take the object gently from him. You can then either throw it for him to chase and pick up, or you can gently reinsert it into his mouth and praise. Do not always throw it for him or else he will pick up only an item that has been thrown. (Should the dog drop the article at any time, SAY NOTHING. Resist the urge to force the article into the dog's mouth. DO NOT raise your voice in any way—this only teaches the dog that you DON'T want the article in his mouth!)

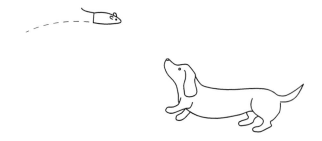

Another spontaneous way that works with many dogs is to toss a soft toy to him. If he catches it (and most dogs will) he has just done a partial retrieve without realizing it. Build on that by using the P's.

Inducive Retrieving

The next method to try is the inducive retrieve. (This is sometimes called play training.) Tease the dog with a soft toy. (Magic Mice sold by Roy

Hunter are ideal!) Pretend that you don't want him to have it—keep turning your back on him. If you have someone to work with, toss the toy back and forth between you and over the dog's head. After a few tosses, one of you should 'accidentally' drop it. If the dog picks it up, run backwards away from him and call him to you. If he doesn't pick the toy up, kick it (the toy, not the dog!) to excite his interest. When he gets to you with the article in his mouth, crouch down and stroke his chest. DO NOT take the article away from him as soon as he gets back! Praise him while he holds the article in his mouth. When you take it from him, do not praise or reward him in any way—he only gets rewarded (praised, petted) for holding it! When he is picking up the article regularly, you can introduce a command. I use PICK IT UP for all nosework or informal retrieves. I use PICK IT UP when I drop my pen, for carrying my newspaper, and when I want my dog to put away his toys! It's practical and it's FUN.

Compulsive Retrieving

The third way to try is the compulsive retrieve which is sometimes referred to as 'formal training'. (This is NOT forced retrieving!) Get your dog used to having his mouth handled. Frequently open his mouth and count his teeth. Massage his lips and gums. Hold his mouth open AND get him used to you holding his mouth shut as well. The more work you put into this, the easier the next stage will be.

Get a six inch length of doweling about one inch in diameter (for a good-sized dog like a Shepherd or Labrador). Touch the dog's shoulders with it, touch his head and touch the outside of his mouth—so he has no fear of the object. Open his jaws and gently insert the dowel behind his canine teeth. (When opening his jaws, insert your finger between his teeth and touch the roof of his mouth—all animals will open their mouths when you do this.) Be careful not to mask the dog's eyes with your hands while opening his mouth— keep your hands below his jaw line. Gently hold his bottom jaw shut, massage his chest with your free hand and whisper sweet nothings in his ear. He may

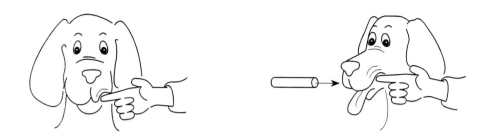

readily accept the situation, he may not. Resist any temptation to tell him off if he tries to dislodge it—just hold it in place gently. As soon as he has stopped struggling, softly say THANK YOU and remove the dowel sideways. Praise him all the time the dowel is in his mouth. DO NOT praise him while you are removing it, or after it has been removed. When re readily accepts the dowel in his mouth, you can introduce the command, PICK IT UP. This command applies anytime you want your dog to hold something in his mouth.

When the dog is happily holding the dowel after you have put it in his mouth, gradually increase the length of time that you allow him to hold it. You can now introduce the next stage—you want him to actually take the article from your hand. If you have praised him enough for holding it, he will want to take it. Hold it in front of his mouth and 'tease' him with it. When you see him start to open his mouth, give your command and gently place it in his mouth and praise. If he drops it, do not get upset! Gently reintroduce it into his mouth and praise. Once the dog is opening his mouth for you, you can gradually start moving the dowel further away. If he will move his head three inches forward to take it, you can build on this by holding it slightly further away each day. At the same time, gradually get the dowel closer to the ground. Occasionally try lifting the dowel UP (so the dog has to jump for it)... he will find this exciting! When you can lay it on the ground, keep your hand under one end to make it easier for him to pick up. Over a period of repetitions, gradually move your hand further away as you command him to PICK IT UP. (It is easier for the dog to pick up the dowel from the ground if one or both ends are raised.) This all may seem long and drawn out to you—many dogs will catch on sooner. We are conditioning the dog slowly and reliably to not only accept retrieving, but to enjoy the process. Remember your P's—a dog will repeat any action he finds rewarding... so make it rewarding!

One the dog is picking things up from the ground, you can gradually place them further away. Notice I said place them. Reserve throwing the article for the inducive training... only very occasionally should you throw the article during formal training. This is to prevent your retrieve from relying solely on the dog's chase instinct.

Take your time. Use ALL of the above methods. Your patience will pay off in the end!

Tug-of-War

A tug-of-war is probably the most stimulating thing we can do as a reward for our dogs. Tug-of-war simulates the "kill" at the end of a hunting expedition. It is very physical, and it is a powerful reaction between dog and handler.

It cannot be used if you are not the true leader of your little 'pack'. If your dog will not give up the item you are tugging with when YOU decide, or, if you cannot stop your dog from pulling you all over the place, then playing 'tug' is not for you. Losing to your dog reaffirms (in the dog's mind) that he is the leader and it is his job to boss you about.

Never allow the dog to initiate the game of tug-of-war. YOU must decide when you are going to play, and YOU must decide when to end the game. It is important to note that AFTER you have won the game, the article MUST be placed out of reach of the dog. If you discard the article after having won the game, and the dog picks it up—the dog sees himself as the winner.

It is not a case of physique or brute strength. A 100 pound woman can easily control a 140 pound Rottweiler while a large man may not be able to control a Yorkshire Terrier. It is a case of who is the true leader—it does not matter what you think, it is the dog's opinion which is important in this case.

It is possible to reverse the position of the dog from leader to follower by using kind methods, without confrontation, by using the dog's natural instincts. There are plenty of books written on this subject. Please consult them for more information. Suffice it to say, just as a man or woman goes further under the thumb of their spouse each time he or she does what the spouse instructs, so a dog gets into the **habit of being obedient** the more we can get him to do anything we tell him to do—and it does not matter if he really enjoys the task we give him or not.

Having decided that you CAN use the 'tug' as a motivation or reward, now we have to teach the dog that he is allowed to play with us in this manner. It is best to start with a soft item or toy. A rolled up piece of denim or toweling is good. (Review the section on retrieving in the appendix.)

Induce the dog to hold the denim in his mouth. Take hold of the protruding ends gently. Remind the dog that he is to maintain his HOLD and very gently ease the ends of the denim away from him. If he lets go, calmly replace the cloth in his mouth and again, after reminding him to keep hold, gently ease the ends toward you. Keep using your informal retrieve command while you put pressure on. Most dogs—with the gentle pull—will do what they do when the lead is pulled—they will pull back. It is an automatic reflex.

One the dog is reliable at resisting your efforts to ease the cloth away from him, you can gradually increase the pressure. In the end (with some dogs) you may be leaning back—putting all your weight on the denim—and your dog will pull determinedly back. When the dog is good at resisting the pressure, you can now incorporate TUG! as a command.

This exercise will NOT cause the dog to refuse to give up items on a formal retrieve such as the dumbbell. The command TUG! means keep hold. The command THANK YOU means let go. You must be deliberate in your action when you actually want to take the item from the dog, and gentle in your action when you want the dog to keep hold.

Having trained your dog on a cloth such as denim, you can now branch out to other materials. A length of leather is ideal—such as the sleeve from an old jacket. (Send the remainder of the jacket to Roy Hunter who uses garment leather for the ears and eyes of his "Magic Mice"—you will not go unrewarded!) You can also use the uppers of a high boot. Dogs like the smell of leather. It is associated with the animal, and thus the 'kill' instinct is brought into action. It is perfectly all right to use your leash in tug-of-war since you always have it with you... provided that your dog only takes a hold of it at your say so AND he releases it immediately when he is told. There are also tugging toys on the market. A rubber hoop is one and there is also a rubber toy designed specifically with a handle for the human at one end and a place for the dog to hold at the other end.

Walking a Dog on Either Side

It is a handy thing to have a dog who will walk with you just as happily on the right as on the left. I use this exercise not only for walking on crowded sidewalks (where I keep my dog out of the way of pedestrians), while enjoying the sport of agility (where the handler should always be on the inside of the 'curve' while the dog is working), and to keep my dog out of traffic while walking along a roadside. In searching for lost articles, the dog should be worked across the wind—which is impossible to do efficiently if your dog must always cling to your left side.

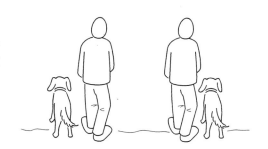

We work a dog across the wind on a search so that the scent of a lost article is blown towards the dog as the dog passes downwind of it. Should you have the dog to your left as you work from the right to the left across a field, your own scent may mask the scent of what you are looking for. You must be able to change sides according to which way you are walking across the field.

Quite simply, hold the dog's leash in your right hand (instead of your left) as close to the collar as you comfortably can so the dog is held close to your right leg. Walk. If the dog tries to duck behind or in front of you to get back to your left side, GENTLY insist that he stay on your right. Praise him. When he accepts the position readily, then introduce your command. I use SIDE to tell my dog to go to my right side and HEEL to tell my dog to go to my left side.

Praise frequently in your initial training. It is not necessary to change your 'footwork' in any way from the way you are already practicing with the dog on your left if you have been doing heelwork.